# Career Guidance and Public Policy

Bridging the Gap

OECD

ORGANISATION FOR ECONOMIC CO-OPERATION AND DEVELOPMENT

# ORGANISATION FOR ECONOMIC CO-OPERATION
# AND DEVELOPMENT

Pursuant to Article 1 of the Convention signed in Paris on 14th December 1960, and which came into force on 30th September 1961, the Organisation for Economic Co-operation and Development (OECD) shall promote policies designed:

- to achieve the highest sustainable economic growth and employment and a rising standard of living in member countries, while maintaining financial stability, and thus to contribute to the development of the world economy;
- to contribute to sound economic expansion in member as well as non-member countries in the process of economic development; and
- to contribute to the expansion of world trade on a multilateral, non-discriminatory basis in accordance with international obligations.

The original member countries of the OECD are Austria, Belgium, Canada, Denmark, France, Germany, Greece, Iceland, Ireland, Italy, Luxembourg, the Netherlands, Norway, Portugal, Spain, Sweden, Switzerland, Turkey, the United Kingdom and the United States. The following countries became members subsequently through accession at the dates indicated hereafter: Japan (28th April 1964), Finland (28th January 1969), Australia (7th June 1971), New Zealand (29th May 1973), Mexico (18th May 1994), the Czech Republic (21st December 1995), Hungary (7th May 1996), Poland (22nd November 1996), Korea (12th December 1996) and the Slovak Republic (14th December 2000). The Commission of the European Communities takes part in the work of the OECD (Article 13 of the OECD Convention).

*Publié en français sous le titre :*

**Orientation professionnelle et politique publique**
COMMENT COMBLER L'ÉCART

# FOREWORD

This publication reports the findings of a review that was begun in early 2001 of career guidance policies in 14 OECD countries. It has looked at how the organisation, management and delivery of career guidance can help to advance some key public policy objectives. In particular, the review has looked at how career guidance services can assist countries to advance lifelong learning goals, and at how career guidance can help in the implementation of active labour market policies. The review has coincided with a growing international interest in the relationship between career guidance and public policy. This interest is reflected in the holding – in 1999 and 2001 – of two international symposia on career guidance and public policy (Canadian Career Development Foundation, 2000 and 2002) and in the conduct of parallel reviews by agencies of the European Commission and by the World Bank. The OECD review has been closely involved with both of these related initiatives.

The review has adopted a broad perspective. Consistent with its focus upon how career guidance can contribute to national lifelong learning policies, it has focused upon career guidance services throughout the lifespan: for young people; for adults; and for the "third age". It has examined career guidance services in a wide range of settings: compulsory schooling; upper secondary education; tertiary education; community settings; public employment services; and the workplace. Its perspective on the stakeholders of career guidance services has also been a broad one, encompassing not only governments, but also employers, trade unions, community organisations, educational institutions, parents, students and career guidance practitioners.

The findings of the review are organised around four main questions:

- Why does career guidance matter for public policy? (Chapters 1 and 2)

- How can career guidance be delivered more effectively? (Chapters 3 to 6)

- How should career guidance be resourced? (Chapters 7 and 8)

- How can strategic leadership be improved? (Chapters 9 and 10)

Details of how the review was conducted are given in Annex 1. This comparative report draws heavily upon the national questionnaires and Country Notes developed in the course of the review. These, together with other key documentation from the review, can be found on the review's web site: *www.oecd.org/edu/careerguidance*.

The national co-ordinators who managed the completion of national questionnaires and the organisation of national visits have been a key to the success of the review. Together with those who have written commissioned papers for the review and the experts who took part in the national visits they have been an important source of much of the thinking that can be found in this report. Details of the national co-ordinators, and of the experts who were involved in the review, are provided in Annex 1. Within the OECD secretariat the review was managed by Richard Sweet and Tony Watts, who were the authors of this comparative report. Administrative assistance was provided by Dianne Fowler, and the project was carried out under the supervision of Abrar Hasan, Head of the Education and Training Policy Division. This report is published under the responsibility of the Secretary-General of the OECD.

# TABLE OF CONTENTS

# OVERVIEW AND KEY CONCLUSIONS

---

### Reading this report

Those reading this report who are pressed for time might like to read only this overview section. It contains both a descriptive summary of the key content of the report, and its key conclusions. Alternatively, they might wish just to read the summaries of key policy conclusions at the beginning of each of the report's ten chapters. Another option is to read only the margin notes on the edge of each page. We hope, of course, that you will have time to read the whole report.

---

## Introduction

As education and employment policies seek to widen choices and to create systems that can respond to varying needs across the lifespan, career guidance becomes increasingly important for public policy. And public policy is important for career guidance: it sets the frameworks for it, and provides most of its funds. However there is a gap between the two. Few career guidance practitioners show a great engagement in policy questions. And few policy-makers have a detailed grasp of how career guidance is organised and delivered. This publication draws upon the experiences of 14 OECD countries to explore ways in which this gap can be bridged. It is organised around four key questions:

- Why does career guidance matter for public policy? (Chapters 1 and 2)

- How can career guidance be delivered more effectively? (Chapters 3 to 6)

- How should career guidance be resourced? (Chapters 7 and 8)

- How can strategic leadership be improved? (Chapters 9 and 10)

## Why does career guidance matter for public policy?

**Chapter 1** describes the expectations, many of which are long-standing, that policy-makers in OECD countries have for career guidance services: to improve the efficiency of education systems and the labour market; and to contribute to social equity. It then sets out the newer challenges that lifelong learning and active labour market policies pose for career guidance: for access to career guidance to be greatly widened; for services to be delivered in far more flexible ways; and yet for these to be done in ways that limit the costs to the public purse. The chapter describes what these newer challenges imply for how career guidance services are organised and provided. At present, services are available largely to limited numbers of groups, at fixed points in life, and are focused upon immediate decisions. The future challenges are: to make a shift so that services focus upon developing career-management skills, as well as upon information provision and immediate decision-making; and to make services universally accessible throughout the lifespan: in ways, in locations and at times that reflect more diverse client needs.

**Chapter 2** points out that there are good conceptual and theoretical arguments in support of the ability of career guidance to help in the implementation of the types of policy objectives that were outlined in Chapter 1. For example the ways in which career guidance is provided might help to better articulate community demand for learning, contribute to higher educational access and completion, and improve the match between labour market supply and demand. Although the empirical evidence in support of this is limited, it is generally positive. This evidence is, however, stronger for its impact upon short-term learning outcomes than upon medium-term behavioural outcomes, and in turn this evidence is stronger than evidence on longer-term impacts. The longer-term evidence is quite weak, and obtaining it will require more and better longitudinal research.

## How can career guidance be delivered more effectively?

**Chapter 3** outlines some of the key policy issues involved in providing career guidance for young people: in schools; for out-of-school and at-risk youth; and in tertiary education. In schools, an approach that sees career guidance only as a personal service, provided by schools themselves, has many limitations. It is costly, and this limits access. It can be too divorced from the labour market and too focused only upon short-term educational decision-making. Where it is combined with personal and study guidance, it is universally given a low priority. Where school funds are tied to student numbers and there is competition between institutions, there can be pressure upon guidance staff to retain students, whether or not this is in their best interests. Some countries, such as Germany, address some of these issues through the use of specialised external services that come into the school to provide personal career guidance.

In addition to addressing these issues, policies for career guidance in schools need to shift away from an approach that focuses only upon immediate educational and occupational choices, and towards a broader approach that also tries to develop career self-management skills: for example the ability to make effective career decisions, and to implement them. This requires an approach that is embedded in the curriculum, and which incorporates learning from experience. Such a strategy requires a whole-of-school approach, and has substantial implications for resource allocation, teacher training and development, and school planning.

Career guidance also has an important role in addressing the needs of students at risk and early school leavers. Many successful examples exist, notably in Scandinavian countries, in which career guidance is embedded in early intervention programmes which incorporate mutual obligation and personal action planning.

The changing face of tertiary education – expanded participation; increased diversity, choice and competition – poses major challenges for career guidance that few countries seem well equipped to handle. In tertiary education such services are generally limited both in scale and in focus, and inconsistent in quality. Comprehensive tertiary careers services are well developed in countries such as Ireland and the United Kingdom, and are growing in other countries, but are generally lacking. The avenues open to governments to improve this situation include the use of performance contracts, as in Finland.

**Chapter 4** describes the main settings in which career guidance is provided for adults, and the policy issues that arise in each of them. In public employment services, which traditionally have been one of the major sources of career guidance for adults, the focus is generally upon short-term employment options rather than longer-term career development. There can be a conflict between the need to restrain expenditure on unemployment benefits and the need to ensure rapid returns to work on the one hand, and the longer-term career development interests of individuals on the other. Within public employment services career guidance generally concentrates upon the unemployed, and services for the employed are much more limited: using self-service methods and with limited opportunities for personal help. And the training and qualifications of those who provide career guidance in public employment services are often at a low level. In Canada career guidance services for adults are commonly contracted out to community groups. This can bring services closer to client needs, but result in services that are fragmented.

Career guidance services, in many countries, are also available in adult education. Here, a major problem is the close links between individual institutions and career guidance, and the need for impartial information and advice is a significant issue. Regionally-based services, such as the adult guidance partnerships in England and the all-age regional careers companies in Wales and Scotland, can be an approach to this issue, as can telephone and web-based services. Systematic feedback from career guidance services can help to improve the match between the supply of adult learning and the demand for it.

Government policy can help to stimulate career guidance provided within enterprises: for example through training levies that include career guidance as allowable expenditure as in Quebec, or through quality-mark schemes such as can be observed in the Netherlands. Innovative arrangements in co-operation with trade unions can be observed in Denmark, Norway and the United Kingdom, and these seem well suited to targeting at least some of the needs of low-qualified workers in the work place.

Significant gaps exist in adults' access to career guidance, and there are indications that demand exceeds the supply of services. In particular, services are more limited for those who are employed, those in small and medium-sized enterprises, and those not in the labour market or not entitled to social security assistance. Much policy attention has been devoted in OECD countries to reforming the retirement age and ways to finance retirement. Yet little attention has been given to policies and programmes that link financial planning to career guidance in order to assist people to make more flexible transitions to retirement. The chapter concludes by suggesting two options for addressing these gaps: strengthening the capacity of public employment services to provide career guidance; and expanding regional partnerships.

**Chapter 5** highlights how innovative and more diverse delivery methods can be used to widen access to career guidance on a more cost-effective basis. These can include group guidance; self-help techniques; the use of community members to deliver parts of programmes; the creation of open-access resource centres; the wider use of support staff; and outreach methods. ICT has a potentially important role to play in widening access, and can be used for purposes that range from the provision of information to raising people's self-awareness and improving their decision-making. Nevertheless there are limitations to the potential uses of ICT in career guidance. These range from bandwidth limitations to lack of training and skills on the part of career guidance staff. Increasing use is also being made of help lines, although call centre technology is under-exploited in many countries. ICT needs to be seen as part of a wider suite of delivery methods, and integrated with, rather than separated from, face-to-face methods. All of the methods outlined in the chapter for delivering career guidance in a more cost-effective way have significant implications for career guidance staffing structures, and for staff qualifications and training arrangements. They also increase the need for screening tools to determine priorities for services and to better match the type of service provided to clients' needs. Such tools exist, but are not widely used.

**Chapter 6** focuses upon career information. It points out that information about the self, about education and training opportunities and about occupations and their characteristics is central to the key theories that underpin career guidance, and that information also plays a central role in how economists treat the efficiency of markets. Good quality career information is thus essential for good quality career guidance. Governments play a central role in funding the collection, organisation, linking, systematising and distribution of career information. At times, as in France, this is through specialised centralised agencies, but more typically it is done through separate ministries, either directly or under contract to private providers. There are also many non-government providers of career information: educational institutions; employers; the media; and the private sector.

If not well co-ordinated between different ministries (particularly education and labour), different sectors of education, and different levels of government, career information can become quite fragmented and non-transparent, making it difficult for people to access. This has implications for both geographical and social mobility. Fragmented career information might suit existing administrative boundaries, but it fails to reflect the types of information that people need to make career decisions. In addition to a lack of integration, common weaknesses in career information include: a failure to include information on labour market supply and demand; delays in capturing changes in the content of occupations or in identifying new occupations; the absence of information on the destinations and labour market outcomes of those completing courses of education and training; a greater emphasis upon educational information than upon occupational and labour market information; and weak links between these two key information domains.

ICT has the potential to overcome many of these problems, particularly lack of integration and poor links between different types of information. However many ICT-based career information systems fail to take advantage of this potential, and simply replicate paper-based systems. Governments have a strong interest in the quality as well as the availability of career information. In the United States standards have been developed to help to maintain and improve career information quality, and these have been a model for the development of similar standards in other countries. To be of real value, career information needs to be not only produced, but also to be disseminated well, and converted into action: policy-makers need to think about how career information can be made meaningful and placed into context.

**How should career guidance be resourced?**

**Chapter 7** addresses the staffing of career guidance services. It begins by pointing out that in nearly all countries information on the size and composition of the career guidance workforce is difficult to obtain. However Canadian and Danish estimates suggest that the number of career guidance practitioners may represent an upper bound of 0.8% of the total labour force.

When assessed against some standard criteria for a profession – such as being able to control labour supply and the existence of clear and lengthy qualification routes – it is clear that in most countries career guidance is not a profession, but an occupation or a role. The training that is provided for career guidance practitioners is rarely both specialised and at tertiary level. Specialised tertiary-level qualifications exist in a few instances – for example Germany's Federal Employment Service and the United Kingdom. More commonly career guidance forms part of more general guidance and counselling training, is limited to short tertiary courses, is in-service, or recruitment is based upon qualifications in fields such as psychology which are related, but too general and insufficient. As a result of limited or insufficient training arrangements, many career guidance practitioners receive no thorough grounding in the basic theories of career guidance, little systematic exposure to its social and economic contexts and purposes, and no systematic applied training in the several methodologies that form the knowledge base of its practice.

While in nearly all countries career guidance practitioners have limited capacity to influence occupational supply, there are examples in countries such as Austria, Canada and the Netherlands of registers of career guidance practitioners being established in order to help to maintain and raise standards of practice. Many countries have a range of associations to represent career guidance practitioners. Often, as in Ireland and Korea, these are poorly linked, making it difficult for policy-makers to relate effectively to the career guidance field.

Occupational structures for the delivery of career guidance need to be strengthened. A priority for policy-makers in most OECD countries should be to create separate, and appropriate, occupational and organisational structures through which career guidance can be delivered, together with associated qualification and training requirements.

The level, content and structure of training courses are central to the capacity of governments to use the types of cost-effective and flexible delivery methods that are needed to widen access to career guidance. Hence the training and qualifications of career guidance practitioners become issues for policy-makers. In many countries, deficiencies are evident in the quality and level of the training that is available, and generally its content shows a number of gaps. Governments need to play a stronger role in shaping the nature of career guidance training and qualifications to remove these barriers to the implementation of key public policy goals.

Comprehensive and modular competency frameworks for the career guidance workforce are a first step in addressing such training deficiencies. Competency frameworks such as the Canadian Standards and Guidelines for Career Development Practitioners can help to bring greater consistency and flexibility to training arrangements. They also have advantages in terms of the management of the career guidance workforce.

**Chapter 8** looks at how career guidance is funded. As with staffing data, information on how much is spent on career guidance is weak in nearly all countries. This arises for a number of reasons, including the low priority that policy-makers have given to collecting such information.

However not all of the problems involved in estimating expenditure are insurmountable. Denmark and Finland, for example, are able to provide estimates of resource use in particular sectors based upon estimates of staff time devoted to guidance. And three countries – Australia, Austria and England – were able to provide sufficient data to enable at least an initial estimate to be made of total government expenditure on career guidance. These range from an annual expenditure of €8.48 per person aged 15-64 in Austria to €23.54 in England. While not directly comparable, the estimates broadly reflect the relative level and intensity of career guidance services in these countries.

How governments fund career guidance has implications for the nature and quality of services. Devolved funding, for example, requires decisions to be made about the residual responsibilities of national governments, and about strategic co-ordination. And it requires policy-makers to consider how to avoid wide variation in the level and quality of services. Staffing formulas can achieve a *de facto* earmarking of funds within devolved funding systems and in systems where block grants are used. Performance contracts and legislative-based entitlements can be other ways to address the issue.

Some career guidance services are contracted out in a number of countries. This can result in cheaper services and in services that are more closely attuned to the needs of particular groups. Whilst some contracting out can be managed by central governments and associated with tight quality requirements, within devolved funding systems it can be associated with wide variation in quality.

Market models are another way in which career guidance can be funded. Relatively strong private markets exist in the publication of career information and in career guidance associated with outplacement services. Some countries, such as the Netherlands, also appear to have limited markets for personal career guidance, paid for by individuals. Information on these markets is sparse. Personal career guidance is difficult to handle through private markets for a number of reasons. Both supply and demand are difficult to specify and define; it is highly variable in its nature; it is often subsumed under other services; and many of those who need it most are least able to afford it. The significant societal benefits that, it has been argued, can flow from well organised career guidance constitute a case for government support for such services, as individual benefits might be harder to capture than in the case of other services. However a wider use of market models could allow government funds to be better targeted on those who can least afford to pay and whose needs are the greatest.

Governments have a role in stimulating markets in order to build overall capacity. They have a role in regulating career guidance markets and in helping to set quality standards. And they have a role in compensating for market failure. There are a number of steps that governments can take that could help to stimulate private markets for career guidance. These include: the wider use of contracting out as a funding mechanism; better specifying the supply of and demand for career guidance in order to make it more transparent; the adoption of more innovative approaches to the financing of career guidance such as linking it to individual learning accounts; and addressing quality standards in order to raise consumer confidence.

**How can strategic leadership be improved?**

**Chapter 9** outlines how policy can have a stronger impact upon the organisation and delivery of career guidance services. Governments have an important role in providing strategic leadership, but need to do so in association with other stakeholders: education and training providers; employers; trade unions; community agencies, students, parents, consumers, and career guidance practitioners. Strong co-operation between education and employment portfolios is particularly important: for example to ensure that educational and occupational information are integrated; and to ensure that a strong labour market perspective is included in schools' career guidance programmes. Whilst mechanisms for leadership and co-ordination are generally weak, some positive initiatives can be seen: for example in Luxembourg, Norway and the United Kingdom.

Evidence and data are important tools for policy-making. While career guidance has a strong research tradition, much of this has concentrated upon theories and techniques, and has had little relevance for policy. Its focus upon both outcomes and costs, for example, has been weak. In addition to better evidence on outcomes and costs, policy-makers in most countries need to obtain improved data on career guidance inputs and processes. Much of this could be obtained by better administrative data. Examples include better information on the characteristics of clients, on the types of services received by different types of clients, and on client satisfaction rates. In the face of some strong evidence gaps (for example on the scale and nature of private markets for career guidance) governments need to improve their national research infrastructure for career guidance. This can be done through a number of concrete steps, including financial support for research institutes that specialise in the link between career guidance and public policy, and the development of academic expertise through the regular commissioning of policy-relevant research.

Legislation is extensively used as a tool to steer career guidance services in countries such as Finland, Spain and the United Kingdom, but is not used at all in others, such as Australia. Where it is used it tends to be rather general in nature. While it provides certain minimum guarantees, it often appears to be quite a weak policy steering tool. Its wider use to define client entitlements could, however, strengthen its value.

Quality standards can be developed for both the processes used to deliver career guidance services, and for the outcomes to be expected of them. They are particularly important in decentralised systems, but also have a key place in centralised systems where governments are the dominant providers. Sometimes the quality standards used to steer career guidance are general industrial standards such as ISO 9000, or part of broader quality standards applying to the sectors (of education, or of employment services) that career guidance services are part of. However examples exist of quality standards that have been developed specifically for career guidance services. In most cases these are voluntary, but they can also be linked to the provision of funds. Generally the link between quality standards and the provision of funds is weak. Career guidance quality standards seem more likely to be effective if they are developed in co-operation with key stakeholders, and are used for continual quality improvement. Quality standards can also be linked to the types of outcomes expected of career guidance services. When phrased in developmental terms, such as the Canadian Blueprint for Lifework Designs, these seem to be particularly attractive in a lifelong learning and active employability context.

Governments can also seek to strengthen the ways in which career guidance services are steered by strengthening the voice of consumers. Steps include client need and satisfaction surveys, and community consultations.

**Chapter 10** outlines the key challenges that face policy-makers in designing lifelong guidance systems, and sets out the choices that have to be made in translating these challenges into practical programmes. In deciding broad priorities for resource allocation, policy-makers should give the first priority to systems that promote career decision-making and career self-management skills, and to systems that produce high quality impartial career information. Policies should not be based upon the assumption that everybody needs intensive personal advice and guidance, but should seek to match levels of personal help, from brief to intensive, to personal needs and circumstances.

A key step must be the identification of gaps in services. These will vary from country to country, and the priorities for filling them will reflect national demographic, educational and economic issues. Nevertheless there are a number of common choices that need to be addressed by policy-makers in all countries. These include deciding when the process should start and how long through the lifespan it should extend. In a lifelong learning context the arguments in favour of it starting during primary school seem strong. At the other end of the lifespan, the arguments are also strong for ensuring that it can help people to plan more flexible transitions between full-time work and retirement.

Policy-makers also need to decide how responsibility for services for young people should be shared. For those who are in school, the strongest arguments are in favour of a shared responsibility between schools and external agencies. In this way the advantages of a developmental approach, a strong labour market focus, and advice that is independent of the interests of particular institutions can be combined. In planning entry to tertiary education, governments should ensure that information on tertiary courses is impartial and adopts a consumer perspective. Governments should also try to ensure that tertiary careers services are comprehensive: including enrolment advice, career development and employability programmes, links with future employers, and job placement. For young people who have dropped out of school early and who are neither in the labour market nor in education the most effective career guidance services are community-based, and part of wider early intervention programmes based around personal action planning.

Where services are provided by external agencies, policy-makers need to decide if these are to be all-age, as in Germany and Wales for example, or age-specific. While age-specific services might appear to have some advantages, many of these can also be provided through all-age services. All-age services have a number of organisational and resource-use advantages. In providing a diverse range of services throughout the lifespan within the one organisational framework, they are potentially more cost-effective, and can avoid resource duplication.

Policy-makers are also faced with a choice between including career guidance as just one element in broader guidance and advisory services, or providing it through specialised career guidance services. The universal experience of the review has been that when included within broadly-focused guidance services career guidance tends to be squeezed by the more immediate and day-to-day personal and study problems of the minority of students with particular problems. Under such circumstances the career guidance and career development needs of the majority tend to be a secondary priority. The importance of providing career guidance through specialised career guidance services is also emphasised by the need for policy-makers to improve the transparency of career guidance in order to make it more accessible.

In seeking to expand adult career guidance services policy-makers can draw upon a number of innovative approaches outlined in this report. These include: a wider role for public employment services; more extended local partnerships; a closer link between financial planning for retirement and career guidance; more innovative and cost-effective delivery methods, with implications for staffing structures and staff training and qualifications; the wider adoption of market-models; and the adoption of more innovative methods to finance career guidance. Some models for providing career guidance to adults already exist. However none of the existing models – whether within education systems, through public employment services, employers, the private market, or the community – is able on its own to meet all needs. A comprehensive approach needs to draw upon several of them, as well as upon more innovative methods, strengthening the case for better strategic co-ordination.

## In conclusion

The creation and management of lifelong guidance systems requires policy-makers to address six major issues, whether in considering career guidance services for young people, for adults, or for both. In most OECD countries these issues have, to date, received minimal attention. They are:

- Ensuring that resource allocation decisions give the first priority to systems that develop career self-management skills and career information, and that delivery systems match levels of personal help, from brief to extensive, to personal needs and circumstances, rather than assuming that everybody needs intensive personal career guidance.

- Ensuring greater diversity in the types of services that are available and in the ways that they are delivered, including greater diversity in staffing structures, wider use of self-help techniques, and a more integrated approach to the use of ICT.

- Working more closely with career guidance practitioners to shape the nature of initial and further education and training qualifications in support of the development of career self-management skills, better career information, and more diverse service delivery.

- Improving the information base for public policy-making, including gathering improved data on the financial and human resources devoted to career guidance, on client need and demand, on the characteristics of clients, on client satisfaction, and on the outcomes and cost-effectiveness of career guidance.

- Developing better quality assurance mechanisms and linking these to the funding of services.

- Developing stronger structures for strategic leadership.

# CHAPTER 1. POLICY CHALLENGES FOR CAREER GUIDANCE

This chapter describes the expectations, many of which are long-standing, that policy-makers in OECD countries have for career guidance services. It then sets out the special challenges that lifelong learning and active labour market policies pose for career guidance, and concludes by describing what these policy challenges imply for how career guidance services are organised and provided.

The chapter's key policy conclusions are that:

♦ While policy-makers in some OECD countries expect career guidance to be centred upon individual goals, in all countries they also expect it to contribute to public policy objectives: making education systems more efficient; contributing to the improved efficiency of the labour market; and helping to improve social equity.

♦ Many of these expectations are long-standing. The progressive adoption of lifelong learning strategies in OECD countries, and an emphasis upon active employability in labour market polices, pose new challenges for career guidance. It needs to shift from being largely available to selected groups, at particular points in life, to being much more widely available throughout the lifespan. And services need to shift from an approach largely focused upon helping people to make immediate decisions through face-to-face interviews, to a broader approach that also encompasses the development of career self-management skills such as the ability to make and implement effective career decisions.

♦ OECD countries need, then, to work towards the development of lifelong guidance systems.

## 1.1. What do policy-makers expect of career guidance[1]?

*There is a gap between career guidance and public policy. This report is about ways to bridge it.*

Public policy has not in the past been of great interest to most career guidance practitioners, whose primary motivation quite properly is a desire to help people. Similarly, the details of how career guidance is provided have often been of limited interest to public policy-makers. Nevertheless public policies set the frameworks for career guidance and provide the funds for much of it. Career guidance becomes increasingly important for public policy as education and employment policies seek to widen individual choices and to create systems that can respond to very different needs throughout life. This report is about how the gap between career guidance and public policy can be bridged.

*Some public policy challenges for career guidance are long-standing.*

Support by public policy-makers for career guidance has traditionally rested upon a belief that it can improve the efficiency and effectiveness of labour markets and educational systems, as well as contribute to social equity. Indeed formal career guidance has its origins in a concern in the early parts of the 20th century to use systematic methods to help underprivileged young people to choose an occupation when they were leaving school and about to look for a job (Parsons, 1909). Some of the policy challenges that career guidance must respond to in OECD countries are long-standing: to improve the knowledge and skills base of the population; to keep unemployment low and ensure that labour supply and demand are in harmony; and to ensure that education and employment opportunities are distributed equitably. Others, as we shall see below, are more recent, and pose new challenges for career guidance.

*Policy-makers in OECD countries expect career guidance to help individuals, but also to serve public policy goals.*

Countries participating in the OECD review of career guidance policies were asked to indicate the key goals and objectives of their career guidance services. They were also asked to indicate the major educational, labour market and social influences that are shaping their career guidance policies. Some countries – Denmark and Norway are examples – made it clear that they expected the goals of career guidance to be centred on the individual: for instance by increasing personal satisfaction, improving career decision-making, or increasing personal development. All countries made it clear that they also expected career guidance to serve a number of important public objectives. And all indicated that their career guidance services are being strongly influenced by current issues and developments in public policy. These public policy goals, issues and developments fall into three broad categories: learning goals; labour market goals; and social equity goals.

---

1. In some countries terms such as "vocational guidance", "vocational counselling", "career counselling", "information, advice and guidance" and "career development" are used to refer to the range of activities that is included here within the term career guidance. In this report career guidance encompasses all of these, and no attempt is made to distinguish between them. Box 1.1 expands on the meaning of the term career guidance. Boxes 1.2 and 1.4 provide examples of the types of activities that it includes.

---

**Box 1.1. What is career guidance?**

Career guidance refers to services intended to assist people, of any age and at any point throughout their lives to make educational, training and occupational choices and to manage their careers. Career guidance helps people to reflect on their ambitions, interests, qualifications and abilities. It helps them to understand the labour market and education systems, and to relate this to what they know about themselves. Comprehensive career guidance tries to teach people to plan and make decisions about work and learning. Career guidance makes information about the labour market and about educational opportunities more accessible by organising it, systematising it, and making it available when and where people need it.

In its contemporary forms, career guidance draws upon a number of disciplines: psychology; education; sociology; and labour economics. Historically, psychology is the major discipline that has under-pinned its theories and methodologies. In particular differential psychology and developmental psychology have had an important influence (Super, 1957; Kuder, 1977; Holland, 1997). One-to-one interviews and psychological testing for many years were seen as its central tools. There are many countries where psychology remains the major entry route.

However in most countries career guidance is now provided by people with a very wide range of training and qualifications. Some are specialists; some are not. Some have had extensive, and expensive, training; others have had very little. Training programmes are still heavily based upon developing skills in providing help in one-to-one interviews. On the other hand, psychological testing now receives a reduced emphasis in many countries as counselling theories have moved from an emphasis upon the practitioner as expert to seeing practitioners as facilitators of individual choice and development.

While personal interviews are still the dominant tool, career guidance includes a wide range of other services: group discussions; printed and electronic information; school lessons;[2] structured experience; telephone advice; on-line help. Career guidance is provided to people in a very wide range of settings: schools and tertiary institutions; public employment services; private guidance providers; enterprises; and community settings.

---

*It is seen as a contribution to the development of human resources...*

**Learning goals**

In some cases, countries expressed the significance of career guidance for education, training and skills development in quite broad terms. For example, Australia, Austria, Canada, Finland, Germany, Ireland, the Netherlands and the United Kingdom made it clear that career guidance is an important part of their approach to lifelong learning. Canada and Korea saw it as one way in which public policy can support the development of human resources.

*...as a way to improve the efficiency of education systems...*

Some countries were more specific about the learning goals that career guidance supports. Austria saw it as one of the ways in which the permeability and effectiveness of educational pathways can be improved. Finland, the Netherlands and Norway saw its importance rising with the growing individualisation and diversification of school programmes. The

---

2.    In schools, it is important to distinguish career guidance, and the career education classes that can be part of it, from vocational education. The one involves preparation for career decision-making. The other involves preparation for entry to a specific employment sector through developing the necessary skills and qualifications. In some countries (*e.g.* Australia, Korea) the two have at times tended to be confused with one another. In Australia, indeed, the growth of vocational courses within schools has to some extent been at the expense of career education programmes, not least because career guidance staff have often been deployed to play significant roles in setting them up and supporting them.

Netherlands argued that career guidance is needed to support the more active approaches to learning that are important in developing lifelong learners. The United Kingdom saw career guidance as an important tool in its efforts to improve levels of basic skills, again an important part of its lifelong learning strategies.

More broadly, it is very common for countries to see career guidance as a tool that can help to improve the efficiency of their education systems. Denmark, Finland, Germany and the Netherlands believed that it can support the attainment of high rates of educational qualification by youth and adults. Austria, Denmark, Finland, Ireland, the Netherlands, Norway and Spain argued that it can help to reduce dropout rates and improve graduation rates.

*...as a tool to help improve the fit between education and the labour market...*

Countries also saw career guidance as a way to improve the interface between education and the labour market. Austria and Norway explicitly said that it is a way to improve the match between the two. Australia, Korea and the United Kingdom saw it as important in improving the school-to-work transition. The Netherlands regarded career guidance as one way to support qualifications upgrading in response to labour market change.

*...and to assist the internationalisation of education.*

Finally, three European countries – Austria, Finland and Germany – saw career guidance as growing in importance as education becomes increasingly internationalised: for example by helping to provide information and advice on international study opportunities. A similar motivation under-pinned the creation in 2003 by the European Commission of a web site portal to provide information on learning opportunities throughout Europe (*www.ploteus.net/ploteus/portal/home.jsp*).

---

### Box 1.2. **Three long-standing approaches**

**Finland's** Employment Office employs some 280 specialised vocational guidance psychologists. Each has a master's degree in psychology, and also completes short in-service training. Many obtain further postgraduate qualifications. Their clients include undecided school leavers, unemployed people, and adults who want to change careers. Clients need to make appointments, and typically have more than one interview. Demand is very high: it is not unusual for people to wait six weeks for an appointment.

**Germany's** Federal Employment Office's career counsellors visit schools, run class talks, and provide small-group guidance and short personal interviews in the penultimate year of compulsory schooling. Many of these counsellors have undertaken a specialised three-year course of study at the Federal College of Public Administration. School classes are taken to the Office's career information centres (BIZ) where they are familiarised with the centre's facilities; they can subsequently re-visit the centre and book longer career counselling interviews at the local employment office.

**Ireland's** secondary schools have one guidance counsellor for every 500 students. Each is required to have a postgraduate diploma in guidance and a teaching qualification. Staffing and qualification levels such as this are quite high by OECD standards. Guidance counsellors are teachers, with a reduced teaching load to provide career advice, to help students with learning difficulties, and to help those with personal problems. Career education classes are not compulsory, but are included in some school programmes.

| | |
|---|---|
| *Policy-makers expect career guidance to contribute to a number of labour market policy objectives.* | *Labour market goals*<br><br>As with learning goals, countries often expressed the importance of career guidance for labour market policies in quite general terms. For example, Australia, Canada, Denmark, Germany and the United Kingdom argued that it is important in helping to improve labour market outcomes or labour market efficiency. Denmark argued that it can help to reduce the effects of labour market destabilisation. Austria, Denmark, Finland, Germany, Korea and Spain indicated that it can help to prevent or reduce unemployment. |
| *For example improving labour mobility…* | There are a number of specific labour market objectives that countries saw career guidance as helping to achieve. For example, Austria and Spain both argued that it can improve labour mobility. Austria, Canada and Luxembourg argued that it can help to improve the match between supply and demand. In a similar vein, Austria, Finland, Germany, Ireland and the Netherlands believed that it can help to improve labour supply and is a way of addressing skill shortages. Canada, Germany, the Netherlands and Spain argued that career guidance can assist active labour market policies by helping to reduce individual dependency upon income support. |
| *…and supporting the ability of the labour market to adjust to change.* | Some countries also argued that career guidance is an important part of policies that support adjustments to the broad changes that are occurring in labour markets. Denmark, Finland, Germany and the Netherlands saw it as important in helping to deal with the effects of an ageing society, or in reducing early retirement. Korea and the United Kingdom saw career guidance as important in helping to support the notion of a lifelong career, as opposed to a lifelong job. Austria, Finland, Germany and Norway argued that it can support the growing internationalisation of the labour market. Canada believed that career guidance can help address the impact of migration on the labour market. |
| *Career guidance is also seen as being able to contribute to equity goals.* | *Social equity goals*<br><br>Somewhat less frequently, countries argued that career guidance can help to achieve a number of social equity goals: both within education and the labour market, and more broadly. Australia and the United Kingdom argued that it can help to promote greater social inclusion. Denmark and Spain argued that it can address the needs of marginalised groups and of the disadvantaged. Finland, Germany and Norway believed that career guidance is important in supporting the social integration of migrants and ethnic minorities. |
| *For example by supporting the disadvantaged or by addressing gender equity.* | Some countries indicated a more specific focus to their social equity goals. Germany and Ireland argued that career guidance can support the integration of the disadvantaged and the poorly qualified in education, and, together with Spain, in employment. Canada argued that it can address growing polarisation in the labour market. |

Some countries focused specifically on gender issues. The Netherlands and Spain believed that career guidance can support rising female labour force participation. Austria, Germany and Norway argued that it can help to address gender segmentation in the labour market.

## 1.2. The special challenges of lifelong learning and active employment policies

*Lifelong learning poses particular challenges for career guidance.*

The steps that many OECD countries are taking to implement lifelong approaches to learning pose particular challenges for career guidance policies and programmes. In broad terms, a commitment to lifelong learning sees learning taking place throughout the lifespan. Just as importantly, it promotes substantial individual control over what is learned, and over the timing, location and mode of learning. It places a strong emphasis not only upon achieving formal skills and qualifications, but also upon developing the motivation to learn and the skills to manage one's own learning (OECD, 2001a).

*More diverse learning systems that increase the potential for individual choice...*

In specific terms, these approaches involve a higher proportion of the population attaining initial educational qualifications at upper secondary and tertiary level. They need more flexible pathways to be created through initial education and training. This requires people to have the knowledge and skills to navigate their way through these pathways and to manage their own learning. And the creation of more learner-driven education systems increases the scope for individual choice in learning. Commitments to broad lifelong learning goals require countries increasingly to make it possible for adults to return to learning, with appropriate assessment and recognition of the knowledge and skills acquired through work and experience.

*...require sophisticated systems of information and advice.*

It is difficult to see how learning systems such as these can operate in the absence of highly developed systems of information and advice, any more than it is possible to see how financial markets could operate in the absence of appropriate information and sources of advice to guide financial investment decisions. Such systems of information and advice are needed both within initial education and within further education and training, and at the interface between both of these and the labour market. Within initial education highly developed information and advice systems are needed to support the development of learning management skills, to support flexible pathways, and to ensure that the benefits of investing in extended education are not lost through making inappropriate choices. Within further education and training they are needed to make sure that adults have the right information and advice to return to study after periods of absence. In particular, well developed information and advice systems are needed to help support people who have low qualifications and low skills. These are the least likely to be able to navigate their way into and through complex education systems, and they are likely, without advice and information, to make poor choices or to drop out of formal learning (OECD, 2003a).

*New thinking about labour market policies also poses challenges for career guidance.*

Closely related to these challenges are ones that emerge from new views of labour market policy. Three developments in approaches to labour market policy, in particular, pose challenges for career guidance: the introduction, in a number of OECD countries, of active, mutual obligation approaches to the payment of unemployment benefits and to welfare dependency; growing interest in the notion of employability as a tool of labour market policy; and the employment implications of ageing societies.

*Active, mutual obligation approaches to unemployment and welfare dependency require a career guidance input.*

### Active, mutual obligation approaches to welfare dependency

With the rise in unemployment levels in OECD countries in the mid-1970s, attention focused upon shifting policy away from the payment of passive unemployment benefits towards more "active" approaches based upon labour market programmes that involve education, training or subsidised employment. Subsequently, approaches towards active labour market policies shifted, and the term came also to connote approaches that involve a mutual obligation. Such mutual obligations involve the unemployed person being required to actively search for work or to undertake training to continue to qualify for unemployment benefits. An emphasis upon earlier intervention to help the unemployed is part of such approaches. A similar approach is part of approaches to the payment of welfare benefits in many OECD countries.

The European Employment Strategy, which was formulated in 1997, is an example of such approaches. It requires member countries to intervene to offer unemployed young people assistance before the end of six months of unemployment. It requires unemployed adults to be offered a similar "fresh start" before reaching twelve months of unemployment: either by being offered training, work practice or another employability measure, or by accompanying individual career guidance (European Commission, 1998).

A key element in many such approaches is the development of an individual action plan, worked out between the benefit recipient and an adviser. A similar approach can be seen in the early intervention programmes that have been introduced, with apparent success, in a number of Nordic countries to deal with early school leavers (OECD, 2000a). If such approaches to unemployment policy and welfare dependency are to be successful, public employment offices and welfare administration centres need greatly improved access to information on education and training opportunities. Their staff need an increased capacity to act in an advisory or guidance role, in addition to a benefit administration, vacancy administration and job placement role.

*The concept of employability also has implications for career guidance if it is to be translated into practical programmes.*

### Employability as a tool of labour market policy

A closely related approach focuses upon the concept of employability. The notion of employability has a number of interpretations (Gazier, 1999). One of these is the more active approach to dealing with unemployment outlined above. A broader view sees employability as a collection of individual attributes such as the ability to find and keep a job, and the capacity to adapt to a changing labour market and new job requirements. Translating such thinking into practical policies and programmes has not gone very far in most OECD countries. However it is hard to see how such thinking about employment policy could be translated into practical programmes without a strong career guidance component.

*And effective policies for ageing societies require mechanisms to advise people on flexible transitions to retirement.*

*The employment implications of ageing societies*

Another challenge that career guidance needs to face is the employment implications of ageing societies. To date much of the policy debate that surrounds ageing societies has focused upon reform to the retirement age and reformed income support arrangements (OECD, 1998a). Debate is emerging on the importance of financial and legislative reforms being accompanied by more flexible working arrangements in the latter periods of life. More flexible working arrangements might allow a sudden shift from full-time work to retirement to be replaced by a more gradual and more flexible transition. Over a longer period this could include options such as part-time work, self employment and voluntary work. Debate is also emerging on the importance of public policies supporting more active ageing, so that additional free time is not used passively, partly to utilise the social contribution of older people, and partly to reduce health expenditure. And it is becoming clear that whether people use their increased leisure actively in their retirement is very much determined by how they use their time when employed (OECD, 2000b).

Alongside the important role that financial planning plays in helping people to prepare for and enjoy their retirement, career guidance has a clear role to play in supporting increased flexibility in time use in the transition from full-time employment to full-time retirement, as well as in helping people better to prepare for the transition (Department for Education and Skills, 2003).

## 1.3.    What do these policy challenges imply for career guidance?

*Traditionally, career guidance has mainly been provided in schools and in public employment services.*

The theoretical basis of career guidance has long emphasised the developmental nature of career decision-making. Yet this has less often been reflected in the ways that services are organised and delivered. In most OECD countries, career guidance has traditionally been provided in two main settings (see Box 1.3). The first of these has been schools, where career guidance has largely focused upon helping young people at the point of leaving school with key decisions such as which occupation or which course of tertiary study to choose. The second main setting for career guidance has been the public employment service, where career guidance has largely focused upon helping the unemployed with immediate job decisions. In both settings face-to-face interviews have been the career guidance method, supplemented by career information, usually in printed form. In both settings information provision and immediate decisions have predominated over the development of career-management skills.

---

**Box 1.3. Where are career guidance practitioners employed?**

Information on where career guidance practitioners are employed helps us to understand what services are provided, and to whom. OECD countries find it very difficult to provide accurate information on the number of career guidance staff and where they are employed (see Chapter 7). The following examples, taken from national questionnaires completed for the OECD review, are indicative:

In **Australia**, an estimated 69% of career guidance personnel are employed in schools, 12% in further education colleges, 6% in universities, and 12% in other settings. The number who provide career guidance in the publicly-funded employment service cannot be estimated with any precision due to the decentralised nature of subcontracted services.

In **Austria**, counting the number of career guidance practitioners is difficult, as most who provide services are not full-time, combining career guidance with other tasks. However it can be estimated that roughly 47% of all practitioners are in schools, 39% in the public employment service, 9% in adult education, and 4% in tertiary education.

In **Canada**, roughly 28% of career guidance practitioners are in employment services and 17% are in schools. 55% are in the community sector.

In **Ireland** 46% of those who provide career guidance are located in secondary schools, 4% in tertiary education, 2% in adult education, and 46% in the two main arms of the public employment service.

---

Inevitably, this emphasis results in gaps in provision. In particular, there is relatively little provision, in most OECD countries, for tertiary students, for employed adults, and for adults not in the labour market.

*The traditional model is not well suited to the wide range of contemporary policy challenges that it is expected to meet.*

There are many variations on these two principal models, and in many countries career guidance is increasingly being provided in a wider range of settings and in more varied ways (as Box 1.4 makes clear). Nevertheless, the traditional model of career guidance does not appear well suited to the full range of contemporary policy challenges that it is expected to meet. The wide range of challenges that policy-makers in OECD countries believe career guidance should be able to address, and in particular the challenge of helping to implement lifelong approaches to learning and active approaches to labour market policy, imply radically different ways of organising and providing career guidance services.

*Significant changes in access and in delivery methods are implied by contemporary policy challenges…*

The policy challenges for career guidance set out above imply that, at the least, career guidance services need to broaden from largely providing assistance with *decisions* at limited and selected points in people's lives to an approach which also encompasses the development of career-management *skills*. In addition, countries need to greatly expand access to career guidance so that it is available to people throughout their lives, and so that it can be available not just to selected groups such as school students or the unemployed, but to all. If this changed emphasis and expanded access were to be achieved solely through the traditional way in which career guidance is provided – face-to-face interviews – there would inevitably be a substantial increase in costs. Both to minimise cost increases, and to meet the needs of a greatly expanded and more diverse range of clients, career guidance needs to be made available much more flexibly in time and space, and to adopt a wider range of delivery methods.

*...if countries are to implement lifelong guidance systems as elements of their lifelong learning and active employment strategies.*

OECD countries need to establish lifelong guidance systems as part of their lifelong learning and active labour market policies. Such systems would have features such as:

- transparency and ease of access over the lifespan, including a capacity to meet the needs of a diverse range of clients;

- particular attention to key transition points over the lifespan;

- flexibility and innovation in service delivery to reflect the differing needs and circumstances of diverse client groups;

- processes to stimulate regular review and planning;

- access to individual guidance by appropriately qualified practitioners for those who need such help, at times when they need it;

- programmes to develop career-management skills;

- opportunities to investigate and experience learning and work options before choosing them;

- assured access to service delivery that is independent of the interests of particular institutions or enterprises;

- access to comprehensive and integrated educational, occupational and labour market information; and

- involvement of relevant stakeholders.

A key aim of the OECD review of national career guidance policies has been to assess how well they are able to meet these criteria.

---

### Box 1.4. **Using innovation to widen access**

**Australia's** national careers web site (*/www.myfuture.edu.au/*) contains information on courses of education and training, on labour market supply and demand at the regional level, on the content of occupations, and on sources of funding for study. Users can explore their personal interests and preferences, and relate these to educational and occupational information. In its first seven months the site was accessed 2.5 million times.

In **Austria** three large career fairs are held each year. They cover vocational training, tertiary education and adult education. They are visited by thousands of people, involve hundreds of professional and trade organisations, employers, trade unions and educational institutions, and are strategically marketed to schools and the community.

**Canada's** public employment services contract many career guidance services to community organisations, which are often seen as more attuned to the needs of particular groups: single parents or Aboriginal people, for example. Some of these organisations focus mainly on career development activities, such as information services, career counselling and job-search workshops. Others have a wider range of education, training and community functions. Some have trained career guidance staff; many do not.

---

Box 1.4. **Using innovation to widen access** *(continued)*

In **England**, the careers service at the University of Leicester used to require all students to make an appointment and have a lengthy interview. During the 1990s student numbers grew by 50% but staff numbers in the careers service declined. This forced a rethink. Now, a drop-in, self-service system in a careers resource centre is the major initial form of contact. Career development programmes are run in all undergraduate classes with each undergraduate department having a careers tutor to act as a first point of contact. Increased use is also made of ICT-based tools.

In **Spain**, the international company Altadis has a career development programme, built around a database of employees' qualifications and descriptions of existing positions in the firm. Those taking part in the programme are interviewed regularly to assess their competencies and aspirations against future business needs. As part of a planned redundancy programme negotiated with the trade unions, Altadis offers career counselling to employees, and has contracted a specialist outplacement firm to provide this service. This firm normally employs psychology or economics graduates.

# CHAPTER 2. IS CAREER GUIDANCE UP TO THE CHALLENGE?

This chapter examines the conceptual and theoretical arguments which suggest that career guidance has a positive contribution to make towards the achievement of many key public policy goals. It presents a framework for thinking of the effects of career guidance, and reviews empirical evidence on its impact.

The chapter's key policy conclusions are that:

- There are good conceptual and theoretical arguments in support of the potential of career guidance to contribute to the achievement of the sorts of public policy goals outlined in Chapter 1. In addition to learning, labour market and equity goals, conceptual and theoretical arguments support its potential to contribute to the development of human capital, broadly defined.

- The empirical literature suggests that evidence for the positive impact of career guidance upon short-term learning outcomes (for example self-awareness, knowledge of opportunities, or decision-making skills) can be treated with considerable confidence. Evidence on the impact of career guidance upon medium-term behavioural outcomes such as educational achievement or dependency upon welfare benefits is less robust, but generally positive. Evidence on longer-term impacts is very limited, and will need better longitudinal research.

## 2.1.    Is career guidance a good idea in principle?

*Conceptual arguments support career guidance...*

Policy-makers in OECD countries have, as we have seen, multiple expectations for career guidance. There are good conceptual and theoretical arguments in support of such expectations.

*...contributing to higher educational access and course completion rates...*

*Learning benefits*

For example, career guidance might help to increase access to learning and educational completion rates by:

- assessing people's learning needs, so that they enrol in programmes that are appropriate to these needs;

- telling potential learners about learning programmes that are available, and putting them in contact with learning providers;

- supporting learners when they are having problems: for example, helping those who are thinking of dropping out to find alternative and more satisfying programmes of study, or to resolve the personal problems that are getting in the way of productive learning; and

- encouraging learning providers to change the way they work in order to meet the needs of new learners: for example, by changing their opening hours, modifying their teaching methods, or developing new courses.

*...and better articulating community demand for learning, and its supply.*

In aggregate, such activities could help to better articulate the scale and nature of the community's demand for learning, as well as its supply. They could help to improve the match between the two. They could increase the transparency of learning systems, and their flexibility in response to consumer demand. In these ways, they could not only increase participation, but also reduce dropout rates.

*This becomes more important as educational choices and alternatives increase.*

The importance of interventions such as these seems to increase as choices within education systems grow, and as the educational choices and labour market consequences that people face become more complex. Recent experience in countries such as Denmark and Finland shows that awareness of the importance of career guidance tends to increase as countries make pathways through education – in particular, through post-compulsory education – more flexible and more individualised. Consumer-driven learning systems require attention to the information and advisory systems needed to make decisions efficient. This increases the importance of career guidance in helping to manage the transitions between education and working life, and transitions from one level of education to another.

*Labour economists have long recognised the role that career guidance can play in labour market efficiency...*

## Labour market benefits

Labour economists and labour market policy-makers have long recognised that career guidance can help improve labour market efficiency (Ginzberg, 1971; Killeen, White and Watts, 1992; Rosen, 1995; Watt, 1996; Autor, 2001; Woods and Frugoli, 2002). This largely rests upon the value of information in improving labour market transparency and flexibility. It also rests upon higher allocative efficiency as the result of a better match between individual talents and qualifications on the one hand and the skills and qualifications demanded by employers on the other. Many of the ways that career guidance could help to improve the efficiency and effectiveness of the labour market are similar to the ways it might help to achieve learning goals. For example, career guidance commonly:

- helps people to understand their interests, abilities and qualifications so that they seek jobs that they are likely to have a chance of obtaining, will enjoy and will do well: and to avoid looking for ones that they might not be able to get, would not enjoy or would not be good at;

- helps people to find out about what is involved in occupations, so that they are more likely to know which ones they might like and be good at;

- helps people to find out about particular jobs that are available and how they can apply for them;

- teaches people how to assess the short- and long-term consequences of particular types of occupational choices;

- makes information about the labour market, and education systems, more accessible by organising it, systematising it, and making it available when and where people need it; and

- teaches people how to search for, understand and evaluate information about occupations.

*...by improving the match between supply and demand, for example...*

In broad terms, interventions such as these seem likely to improve the flexibility and transparency of the labour market. For example, they could help to improve the match between supply and demand by helping people to search for a better fit between their talents and qualifications and available work opportunities. Unemployment could be reduced if such interventions helped to reduce the incidence of voluntary employment terminations or periods of job search (thus reducing frictional unemployment); or if they encouraged those made redundant to improve their qualifications or to seek new types of work in different regions (thus addressing structural unemployment).

*...and contributing to the development of employability.*

Career guidance also has the capacity to contribute to the development of employability: through assisting the unemployed to assess their training needs; through helping those on welfare benefits to plan how they can re-enter the labour force; and through helping people to develop the skills needed to manage their careers.

*Career guidance can also be argued to make a contribution to equity through its role in maximising the use of people's talents, regardless of their background.*

### Equity benefits

There are also strong conceptual arguments in support of the contribution that career guidance can make to social equity. Many career guidance activities attempt to maximise the use that people make of their talents, regardless of their gender, social background or ethnic origin. Disadvantaged groups are likely to be less familiar with educational and labour market information than more advantaged groups. They may be more under-confident in, unskilled in, or unused to negotiating access to complex learning systems. They may need more help in finding opportunities that can maximise their talents, and in overcoming barriers to accessing these opportunities.

If targeted on disadvantaged groups, as some programmes and services are in OECD countries, career guidance seems to have the potential to contribute to the implementation of many national equity goals: the integration of immigrants and refugees into employment and training; reducing gender segmentation in the labour market; reducing the impact of family advantage upon educational and labour market outcomes; reducing the impact of these factors upon tracking within education systems; increasing social cohesion.

*Career guidance also has the potential to contribute to the development of human capital, broadly defined.*

### Human capital benefits

People's knowledge and skills play a strong role in economic growth in OECD countries. The importance of human capital as a source of economic growth appears to be increasing (OECD, 2000c; OECD, 2001b). Traditionally human capital has been defined largely in terms of people's productive capacity and characteristics: in other words in terms of "skills", broadly defined. Newer and wider ways of thinking about human capital (OECD, 2002) point out that less than half of earnings variation in OECD countries can be accounted for by educational qualifications and readily measurable skills. It argues that a significant part of the remainder may be explained by people's ability to build, and to manage, their skills. The characteristics that are important in the development of human capital include the ability to acquire skills: in other words, to learn, to identify one's learning needs, and to manage one's learning. They also include the ability to understand how best to use these skills. Included in this category are career planning, job search and career-management skills. There is a close harmony between this wider view of human capital and some notions of employability. Seen in this wider context, it seems that many aspects of career guidance have the potential to contribute significantly to national policies for the development of human capital.

## 2.2. Is career guidance effective in practice?

*While the model for evaluating career guidance is a complex one...*

The model for evaluating career guidance properly is a very complex one (Maguire and Killeen, 2003). Types of clients and their needs and problems vary widely. The help that they receive is also very diverse, co-exists with other interventions and influences, and is often quite brief. Outcomes, both intended and unintended, behavioural and attitudinal, short- and long-term can also vary widely. Obtaining clear answers about impacts under these circumstances requires large-scale research with complex experimental designs and statistical controls. Such research is lengthy and expensive. To date limited studies have been conducted.

*...career guidance has been identified as one element in a number of effective policies.*

Evaluation studies have, however, identified guidance services as among the key features of effective policy approaches in a number of areas, even if their separate contribution cannot readily be disentangled. It has been found, for example, to be an element of effective approaches to: labour market programmes (Martin, 1998; OECD, 1999); welfare-to-work programmes (General Accounting Office, 1999; McIntyre and Robins, 1999); secondary schooling (Lapan *et al.*, 1997); and the transition from school to work (OECD, 2000a).

*Its effects can be thought of at the individual level...*

### A framework for thinking of potential effects

The potential effects of career guidance can be thought of at the individual, organisational and societal levels. At the *individual level*, potential benefits could result from people being better able to manage their choices of learning and work, and to maximise their potential. At the *organisational* level, potential benefits could flow to education and training providers if learners were assisted to identify and enter learning programmes which meet their needs and aspirations. And they could flow to employers if career guidance resulted in a supply of job applicants whose talents and motivations were matched to employers' requirements.

*...the organisational level...*

*...and the societal level.*

Benefits could result at the *societal* level if career guidance leads to greater efficiency in the allocation of human resources: for example by enhancing the motivation of learners and workers; reducing drop-outs from education and training; reducing mismatches between labour supply and demand; encouraging upskilling of the workforce; reducing the incidence of floundering between job transitions; and thus improving the ways that learning and labour markets operate. Social benefits could also result if career guidance helped to widen access to learning and work opportunities (both helping people to avoid social exclusion and helping the excluded to gain access to learning and work), thus enhancing social equity. Career guidance services might also be thought of as reinforcing the value attached in democratic societies to the right of individuals to make free choices about their own lives.

*Effects can range from the immediate to the longer-term.*

These potential effects can be thought of as operating at three stages: *immediate* attitudinal changes and increased knowledge; *intermediate* behavioural changes for example through improved search efficiency and persistence, or through entering a particular career path, course or job as a result of career guidance; and *longer-term* outcomes such as success and satisfaction.

*Most evaluations to date have concentrated on learning outcomes.*

*Learning outcomes*

Most of the existing evaluation evidence relates to learning outcomes. There are two main reasons:

- It is appropriate. Learning outcomes directly represent the aims of career guidance interventions. Mostly, career guidance is concerned not to tell people what to do but to help them acquire knowledge, skills and attitudes which will help them to make better career choices and transitions.

- It is fairly easy to do. Since learning outcomes are immediate, they are relatively easy and cheap to measure. Studies of longer-term outcomes are more complex and expensive to mount, and more subject to contamination from extraneous factors.

A review by Killeen and Kidd (1991) of 40 (mainly United States) studies divided the learning outcomes from career guidance into six main categories:

- precursors: attitudinal factors which facilitate rational decision-making such as reduced decision-anxiety;

- self-awareness: learning about self;

- opportunity-awareness: learning about opportunities and options;

- decision-making skills: learning rational decision-making skills and strategies;

- transition skills: learning skills for implementing decisions (including job-search skills and interview skills);

- certainty of decision.

*Positive impacts upon learning outcomes are reported in many studies.*

The findings were overwhelmingly positive: of the 40 studies, only four reported no gains in the categories identified, 30 reported wholly positive results, and gains were reported in each category more often than null results. Also, positive results were reported for each main type of guidance intervention: classes and courses, workshops and groups, individual guidance, test interpretation and feedback, experience-based interventions, and multi-method interventions.

Similar conclusions have been found in more extensive and more rigorous United States meta-analyses of good-quality controlled studies by Spokane and Oliver (1983), by Oliver and Spokane (1988) and by Whiston, Sexton and Lasoff (1998). The latter study concluded that:

- career interventions are effective with most age-groups;

- individual guidance has the biggest effect, followed by group counselling and classroom interventions;

- counsellor-free interventions have the smallest effect sizes;

- computer-delivered interventions are the most cost-effective.

A review of the impact of career interventions by Prideaux *et al.* (2000) which included both meta-analyses and individual studies, concluded that:

> "Career intervention studies have displayed almost unanimous support for the provision of some kind of career counselling or education for both adolescents and adult samples. Programs that aim to assist people in a variety of career-related activities including career decision making, career exploration, career maturity, and career self-efficacy have generally shown positive effects" (p. 236).

*The behavioural effects of career guidance are hard to assess.*

*Behavioural outcomes*

Studies of behavioural outcomes require a follow-up design, which raises a number of difficulties. The effects may not be visible for some time. But the longer the time that elapses, the more other factors come into play. Studies with control groups are particularly difficult to sustain over extended periods: contact cannot be indefinitely extended, nor guidance indefinitely denied.

*However a limited number of studies suggest positive effects on behaviour: for example on participation in learning...*

A number of studies have been carried out to determine the extent to which guidance interventions result in behavioural outcomes such as participation in education and training programmes. Studies in the United Kingdom have demonstrated significant positive effects both for employed (Killeen and White, 2000) and for unemployed adults (Killeen, 1996a). An Australian study showed that even a modest career counselling intervention with a very disadvantaged group of unemployed individuals led to a significant increase in participation in learning (Breunig *et al.*, 2003). A Finnish study found that intensive guidance courses were more effective than subsidised employment or training in getting unemployed people off the unemployment register and into unsubsidised employment (Vuori and Vesalainen, 1999).

*...on reduced welfare payment receipt...*

The main evidence published to date on the intermediate economic benefits of career guidance interventions relative to their economic costs was a series of United States studies on the effectiveness of Job Clubs. Six months after participation, mean welfare payments had reduced by 48% for Job Club participants but only by 15% for controls. This exceeded the cost per placement and therefore indicated a net saving (Azrin *et al.*, 1980, 1981).

*...and on educational achievement.*

Not all career guidance is designed to lead to immediate decisions. Career education programmes in schools, for example, have longer-term aims. However evaluations of their impact have largely focused upon intermediate effects: on educational motivation and hence on academic attainment (Killeen, Sammons and Watts, 1999). In the United States, career education programmes have shown some modest but positive effects on various measures of academic attainment (Evans and Burck,

1992). Similarly, comprehensive guidance programmes in schools have been shown to have a modest but significant additive effect on self-reported grades as well as on the perceived value of education as an investment for the future (Lapan, Gysbers and Sun, 1997).

***Evidence on longer-term impacts is very limited.***

*Long-term outcomes*

On long-term outcomes, the available evidence is very limited. The methodological difficulties encountered in studies of behavioural outcomes are multiplied in the case of long-term longitudinal studies. Sample sizes are not easy to sustain, and effect sizes inevitably decline as other factors intervene. Such studies are very costly to mount, and difficult to execute satisfactorily.

A key difficulty is defining the intervention whose impact is being measured. If this is a single intervention viewed as an event – a single career counselling interview, for example – it seems unrealistic to expect large effects to be sustained over a long period of time. If on the other hand attention is focused on the effect of a series of interventions viewed as a process, the problems of defining and controlling these interventions, and of identifying control groups which have had access to no such interventions, become much more difficult to solve. These problems grow as career guidance becomes more diverse in its nature.

Of some historical interest in this respect is a series of studies, mainly conducted in the 1920s and 1930s, which examined the effectiveness of so-called scientific guidance based on the use of psychometric tests. These studies demonstrated that those who entered jobs in line with the recommendations based on such guidance were more satisfied with, and more stable in, their jobs, than those in jobs differing from the recommendation. They also showed that in controlled trials, the effect of the guidance was to raise the perceived suitability of their jobs and to reduce job turnover (for a review of these studies, see Watts and Kidd, 1978).

***Better, and more longitudinal, research is needed.***

*Future research needs*

In general, the evidence on the benefits of career guidance is limited but positive. It indicates that evidence for its positive impact upon short-term learning, motivational and attitudinal outcomes can be treated with a high degree of confidence, and in the case of its impact upon actual behaviour with moderate confidence. However evidence on its impact upon long-term individual outcomes, and hence upon economic outcomes, is very limited. If more definitive long-term evidence is required by policy-makers, the studies to establish such evidence need to be mounted. In particular, if longitudinal studies could explore the relationship between immediate learning outcomes and longer-term outcomes, and if positive connections between them were to be established, the learning outcomes could thereafter be regarded not only as being of value in their own right but also as proxies for longer-term outcomes (Killeen, White and Watts,

1992). To date, no such studies have been conducted. In addition, few studies have been conducted which directly relate costs to benefits. More such studies are needed, with different populations and under diverse conditions.

*Newer delivery models also need to be evaluated.*

A further important issue is that most evaluations to date have studied types of career guidance that may be diminishing in relative importance (one-to-one face-to-face counselling, for example). Few studies have yet been conducted of the impact of service delivery models incorporating extensive use of client self-service and of information and communication technologies.[1] This is an example of the need for more sustained research on the interaction between types of treatment and types of outcomes.

---

1.      These newer delivery models also have implications for the collection of basic data on who the clients of career guidance services are. This point is raised again in Section 9.2.

# CHAPTER 3. MEETING THE CAREER GUIDANCE NEEDS OF YOUNG PEOPLE

This chapter outlines some of the key policy issues involved in providing career guidance for young people: in schools; for out-of-school and at-risk youth; and in tertiary education.

The chapter's key policy conclusions are that:

♦ When career guidance in schools is delivered as a personal service, through personal interviews, it is expensive and access to it is limited. It can also be too remote from the labour market when provided by schools themselves, too subordinate to personal and study guidance if provided by those who are not career guidance specialists, and too linked to the self-interest of particular institutions. Providing it through specialised external career guidance agencies that visit the school can help to overcome some of these problems. There is, though, a risk that too much dependence on such agencies will reinforce the concept of career guidance as a service and weaken links with the curriculum. Links with such agencies should be complementary to, rather than a substitute for, programmes inside the school.

♦ To develop students' career self-management and career decision-making skills, an approach based upon personal interviews is not enough. It needs to be supplemented by a developmental approach, embedded in the curriculum and with a strong experiential component. Such programmes need to involve community members as well as school staff. They have significant implications for the organisation of the whole school: the curriculum; resource allocation; and teachers' skills.

♦ Career guidance is almost invariably a component of the most successful programmes for out-of-school youth. Such programmes work best when they are located in the community, highly individualised in their approach, and involve mutual obligations and individual action-planning.

♦ Increasing rates of participation in tertiary education in OECD countries have coincided with the development of a more diverse and competitive tertiary education sector whose links to the labour market have become both more extensive and more diffuse. These developments have implications for the provision of tertiary education career guidance services that few countries have yet addressed adequately. In order to improve tertiary careers services, broadening their scope and application, governments have a number of policy levers available, including performance contracts and wider use of public analysis and debate.

## 3.1.   Meeting needs in schools

*Lifelong learning transforms the role of guidance in schools.*

The policy challenges for career guidance outlined in Chapter 1 have significant implications for schools. They must: ensure that *all* students can access career guidance, not just a few; extend career guidance beyond a personal service approach focused upon immediate occupational and tertiary education decisions; allow all young people, as part of the curriculum, to develop the skills to manage their progression in learning and work throughout their lives; and incorporate an experiential component, closely linked to the labour market and the world of work.

*Previously, guidance in schools has been viewed as a personal service...*

*Career guidance as a personal service*

Traditionally, career guidance in schools has been viewed largely as a personal service, provided at key decision points, and a support to the curriculum rather than part of it. It has mainly been delivered through personal interviews, sometimes supported by psychometric testing. This has made it expensive to provide to large numbers, and so has limited its availability.

*...focused mainly on educational choices...*

Personal career guidance services in schools have commonly suffered from further constraints. The focus has tended to be on educational decision-making, often with little attention to the occupational and longer-term career choices that flow from particular educational pathways. In particular, where career guidance services are wholly school-based, links with the labour market can be weak. And those who are planning to enter tertiary education may receive greater attention than the job-bound: Figure 3.1 shows that, at the upper secondary level, this is the case in many countries: Belgium (Flemish Community), Denmark, Finland, Hungary, Ireland, Korea, Mexico, Norway and Switzerland.

*...often subsumed under personal counselling...*

Such problems are made worse if, as in countries such as Canada, Ireland and Norway, guidance counsellors have to deal with personal and social guidance as well as educational and vocational guidance. The two areas of work require rather different skills and resources. Career guidance, for example, requires regular updating to keep in touch with changes in the education system and the labour market. This may not be given sufficient attention within an integrated model. The universal experience appears to be that attention to the educational and vocational guidance needs of all students tends to get squeezed by attention to the personal and social guidance needs of those few students with particular difficulties:

- In Canada, a survey of school guidance counsellors in 1994 found that 61% named personal crisis counselling as one of their top time-consuming tasks, whereas only 32% named career planning and only 25% educational planning (cited in Canada questionnaire response).

- In Norway, some guidance counsellors spend up to 80% of their time dealing with pressing personal and social matters (Teig, 2000).

- The tendency for personal and study counselling to squeeze attention to career guidance within holistic roles has also been observed in the current review in Australia (Queensland), Ireland and Korea, as well as in other countries. A recent American survey of high school guidance services reveals that helping students with their school academic achievement is the most emphasised goal of school guidance programmes, and that schools are least likely to report that the most emphasised goal is helping students to plan and prepare for their work roles after high school. The survey reveals that the activity on which guidance staff spend most time is the choice and scheduling of high school courses (National Center for Educational Statistics, 2003; see also Grubb, 2002b, p. 14).

Figure 3.1. **Percentage of upper secondary students in academic and vocational programmes who receive individual career counselling, 2002**

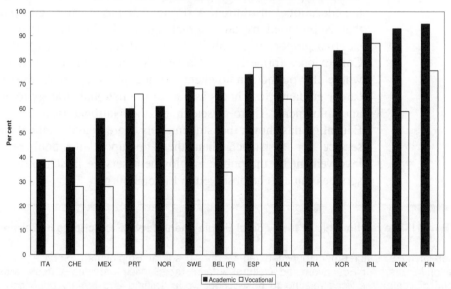

*Note*: Academic programmes refer to those general education programmes classified as 3-AG in ISCED97 *i.e.* those designed to lead to tertiary education. Vocational programmes refer to those classified as 3-BV or 3-CV in ISCED97 *i.e.* non-academic (pre-) vocational programmes. However in the case of Finland, Italy and Sweden the reference is to those programmes classified as 3-AV in ISCED97 *i.e.* academic (pre-) vocational programmes.

*Source*: OECD International Survey of Upper Secondary Schools.

This tendency is partly because the personal and social needs of students with difficulties are often more demanding, particularly if they are causing disruption within the school. It may also be strengthened by the personal predilections of the guidance counsellors, which may have been reinforced by their training. Reflecting such concerns, Norway has set up a three-year trial project to explore how responsibility for educational and vocational guidance on the one hand, and personal and social counselling on the other, might be split by attaching them to different roles (with good referral links between them). Countries in which schools already split the two roles include Australia (New South Wales) and the Netherlands.

*...and possibly under some pressure to serve the interests of the school rather than the student.*

A further problem with school-based guidance services is that they may be under pressure to place the institutional needs of their school before the needs of students. These pressures often operate in subtle, subconscious ways. They are particularly evident in systems where school funding is linked to the recruitment and retention of students. In such cases, guidance services may tend to promote the interests of their institution, even in cases where it is not in the interests of a student to enrol or remain there. Such pressures have been noted in a number of countries in the review, including Denmark, the Netherlands and the United Kingdom.

*Some countries accordingly provide career guidance from outside the school.*

A response in some countries to these various issues has been for personal career guidance to be provided by an agency based outside the school. The potential advantages of this include the possibility of career guidance having closer links to the labour market, the likelihood that career guidance will have a clear identity, separate from other forms of guidance, and the increased possibility that guidance will be independent of the interests of the educational institution. A strong example of career guidance in schools that is provided by an external agency is Germany (Box 3.1). Strong external support to schools is also provided in the United Kingdom through Connexions, formerly the Careers Service, and in the Czech Republic where the public employment service plays a strong role in providing career guidance to schools as part of the national strategy to address youth unemployment. There, research by the National Institute of Vocational Education has shown that students rely more heavily upon the employment service for assistance than they do upon in-school services. Some involvement by the public employment service in school career guidance services can also be observed in Luxembourg.

---

Box 3.1. **The relationship of the Federal Employment Service to schools in Germany**

As the result of a 1971 agreement between the German Federal Employment Service and the Standing Conference of Ministers of Education and Cultural Affairs, the Service provides schools with information, guidance and placement services relating to post-school work, training and tertiary education options. This complements the school's responsibilities for vocational orientation both within the curriculum and through work-experience programmes, and for guidance on educational choices within the school.

Career counsellors visit the school to run a two-hour session with each class in the penultimate year of compulsory schooling. They are also available for further class sessions, for small-group guidance sessions or for short career counselling interviews. Classes are then taken to the service's career information centre (BIZ), and can re-visit the centre individually for longer interviews. The service's career counsellors also commonly attend parents' evenings and help to organise other events like career fairs. There are specialist career counsellors for *Abitur* students. The Federal Employment Service also provides a range of free information (magazines, handbooks, brochures, CD-ROMs and on-line information) for all school students and for *Arbeitslehre* teachers. Co-operation is fostered by a Standing Contact Commission with representatives of both sides. In addition, supplementary agreements have been made at *Länder* level. The detailed arrangements are negotiated annually at local level between the local labour office (*Arbeitsamt*) and schools.

---

In several countries links with such external agencies have been weakened in recent years:

- In Austria, Canada, Denmark and Norway, staff from the employment service used to visit schools fairly regularly. Now, such links are commonly confined to occasional events like careers fairs. Although career information may be distributed to schools, links which might help to activate and flesh out this information are largely absent.

- In the Netherlands, the former state-funded guidance offices were merged with other education-work brokerage organisations into 16 regional guidance offices (AOBs) which were expected to provide demand-based guidance services to schools and other organisations. Their government subsidies were gradually reduced, and the funds passed to the schools, which were free to purchase services from the AOBs or elsewhere, or to retain the money and provide the services themselves. Many preferred the latter course. As a result, the number of AOBs has been reduced, through mergers, takeovers and bankruptcies, from 16 to 3, with the number of staff shrinking from around 1 800 in the mid-1980s to around 300 by the end of the 1990s (see Meijers, 2001).

- In New Zealand, a more modest form of the same policy has been followed, with some centrally contracted services continuing to be funded from Careers Services (a government agency) but with additional school-managed funding being provided for additional services which can be purchased on a contestable basis from Careers Services or from private providers (see Oakes and von Dadelszen, 2000).

On the other hand, a number of countries are considering setting up a new range of external agencies. In Australia, the federal Government is introducing Career and Transition Pilots under which 30 career and transition advisers will work with schools, local communities, young people and their families. In Denmark, the possibility is being explored of setting up 50 new cross-sectoral centres at the interface between the *folkeskole* and the various forms of youth education. In Korea, there are plans to establish centres in each province, to provide a resource centre for schools as well as a place where both young people and adults could go for independent career counselling.

*Such services should reinforce, not replace, school-based programmes.*

Services based outside the school can considerably strengthen careers programmes in schools. There is, though, a risk that too much dependence on such agencies will reinforce the concept of career guidance as a service and weaken links with the curriculum. Links with such agencies should be complementary to, rather than a substitute for, programmes inside the school.

*Programmes that are part of the curriculum are growing in importance.*

### Career guidance in the curriculum

In recent years there has been a trend for career guidance based upon personal interviews to be supplemented with a curriculum-based approach. An emphasis upon lifelong learning and sustained employability greatly enhances the case for such an approach.

*These include career education programmes, which vary in content...*

As Annex 2 illustrates, most countries now include programmes of career education within the curriculum. These vary in content. Some (*arbeitslehre* in Germany, for example) focus mainly on understanding the world of work and its demands. Most, however, also include attention to self-awareness and the development of skills for making decisions and managing transitions. In a lifelong context, this broader approach is highly desirable.

*...in structure...*

Career education programmes also vary in their structure. Three broad patterns can be distinguished: *stand-alone* programmes that are run as a separate course; programmes that are *subsumed*, for example included as one strand of a course in personal, social and health education, or in social studies; and programmes that are *infused* within most or all subjects across the curriculum. In some countries (for example Australia, Austria, the Czech Republic and the United Kingdom) more than one of these patterns can be seen. Often this is because of the autonomy that schools are given to decide which model to select.

In many cases, as the examples in Annex 2 show, the programmes are mandatory. This is the case in Austria, in some Canadian provinces, in the Czech Republic, in Denmark, in Finland, mostly in Germany, in the Netherlands, in principle in Norway, in Spain, and in the United Kingdom. In some of the Canadian provinces it leads to credits that are needed for graduation. However in other cases, such as Ireland, Korea and Luxembourg, it can be left to the individual school to decide whether to offer it or not.

Where career education is mandatory, its quality is easier to monitor in its stand-alone or subsumed forms. With the infusion model, provision can be patchy, disconnected and often invisible to the student. At times it can be adopted for reasons that have little to do with the needs of students. In Austria, for example, it was adopted only because of resistance by teachers to time being taken away from the teaching of their subjects. Experience in Austria and Norway shows that the infusion model requires a high level of co-ordination and support to be effective. And it needs some separate provision where the student is helped to make personal sense of the bits and to pull them together. In the Netherlands, a previous requirement for all teachers to include career education in their teaching has been largely withdrawn in order to reduce the load on teachers.

*...in location...*

School systems vary in the grades in which career education is located. Annex 2 suggests that the most common approach is to concentrate career education in lower secondary education. There are exceptions: in Canada (British Columbia and Ontario), the Czech Republic, Finland and Spain it extends into upper secondary education. In Canada (British Columbia and Ontario), the Czech Republic and Denmark it begins in primary school. The dominant pattern reflects a common assumption that the key career-related decisions are made at the end of compulsory schooling. Such an assumption might have had some validity when the end of compulsory education represented the main point of transition from school to the labour market, or from school to very specific occupational preparation. However this is less and less the case in nearly all OECD countries. In the context of lifelong learning, the case for starting in primary school is strong. Box 3.2 describes an innovative career education curriculum resource that can be applied from grade 3 through to grade 12: it is operating in ten OECD countries.

---

#### Box 3.2. **The Real Game**

The Real Game is a career development programme that involves role playing and simulation. Through interactive and experiential exercises in the classroom, it allows students to learn about adult life and work roles and engage in career and educational planning. It helps them to understand how their choices, including decisions about their school work, may affect their lives as adults. Although presented as a game, it contains defined learning objectives and clear performance indicators. The Real Game normally takes between 18 and 23 hours of class time to complete. This can be played in an intensive week, or extended over longer periods such as a term or a full school year. Other career guidance resources can be linked to it, and it can involve parents, people from the community, and more than one teacher.

The Real Game involves six developmentally-sequenced games that can be played in grades 3-4, 5-6, 7-8, 9-10 and 11-12, as well as with adults. To illustrate these: in the grade 3-4 game, students may prepare and rehearse responses to questions about services and businesses in their town or neighbourhood; in the grade 7-8 game they may reflect on their attitudes to the roles of men and women in society, or brainstorm how they would respond to being unemployed; in the grade 11-12 game they may simulate experiences encountered three years after leaving school, or interview one another to see if they have the education, experience and skills required for a particular career.

The Real Game was launched in Canada in 1996 after extensive development involving over 5 000 students, parents, teachers and career guidance practitioners. It has since been extended under licence to nine other countries: Australia, Denmark, France, Germany, Hungary, the Netherlands, New Zealand, the United Kingdom, and the United States. Before being launched in a country, each game in the series undergoes development, piloting and evaluation, guided by an international advisory group. This is complemented by national advisory committees. The Real Game Series is funded by Human Resources Development Canada under the understanding that all programmes in the series will be fully self-sustaining once launched. Further information can be obtained at *www.realgame.com/*. Edwards *et al.* (1999) provide an evaluation of the United Kingdom trials of the game for 12-13 year-olds.

---

*...and in the students they include.*

Where career education is located in the curriculum determines which students are involved. In most cases, all students are. In Germany, however, where students are normally divided into different types of school between the ages of 10 and 12, *arbeitslehre* is less commonly provided to students in the *gymnasium* than to those in the *hauptschule* or *realschule*. In Ireland, career education is mandated for students in the Leaving Certificate Vocational Programme, and may also be included in Transition Year programmes, but may not be offered to other students. In the Netherlands it is compulsory in pre-vocational education: "orientation towards learning and working" is included in the upper forms of all general subjects, and "orientation towards the sector" in all vocational subjects. In general education, however, "orientation on continued education" is an optional part of the so-called "free space" periods, and (as its name suggests) focuses more on educational choices than on their longer-term career implications.

*Career education
needs to be linked to
work experience.*

Career education programmes need to be closely and actively linked to the world of work and to post-school educational options. In many countries, the curriculum includes work experience, work shadowing, work visits, and work simulation such as mini-enterprises. For example in Australia and the United Kingdom, it is usual (though not mandatory) for students to have a one- or two-week work-experience placement before major subject choices are made. In Denmark and Norway, most students have at least two one-week work-experience placements. In other countries such opportunities are much more limited: this is the case in Austria, Ireland, Korea and the Netherlands, for example. Another approach, used in countries like the United Kingdom and the United States (Grubb, 2002a), has been to use mentoring schemes which match adults with young people on a longer-term basis. These can be used for various purposes, including coaching for career plans. As well as work experience, some school systems arrange for students to "taste" particular educational opportunities before making decisions. Well-developed arrangements for this exist in Denmark.

*Profiling and
portfolio systems can
be a way to develop
career-management
skills.*

A potentially important role is played by profiling and portfolio systems, designed to encourage students to manage their own learning and to see its relationship with their career plans. These programmes can start in primary school: for example in the Netherlands, some primary schools in Rotterdam have started to plan for the introduction of a portfolio system, broadly similar to those being introduced into some secondary schools. Some systems are strongly career-related. In Australia (New South Wales), an Employment Related Skills Logbook enables students to identify the work-related competencies they are developing through their various school subjects and to relate these to their career planning. Similar systems in Canada (Ontario) and Denmark are described in Box 3.3.

---

**Box 3.3. Portfolio systems in Canada and Denmark**

In **Canada** (Ontario), the "Choices into Action" programme requires all students to develop and maintain an academic and career portfolio, and in grades 7-12 also to complete annual education plans. To support this process, schools are required, at least in grades 7-11, to assign teachers to act as advisers. They regularly timetable group sessions of at least 30 minutes per week with the students (usually numbering between 12 and 20) for whom they are responsible.

In **Denmark**, students must develop individual education plans from grade 6, in preparation for choice of subject options. As part of this, they are expected to see the guidance counsellor for one individual session in grades 6 and 7, and for two sessions in grades 8 and 9. The process is supported by an education book: a personal document in which pupils record their achievements and their developing interests and aims. The plans themselves have to be signed by the pupil, a parent and the guidance counsellor. This system offers a clear entitlement: an assurance that each pupil will be seen singly on a number of occasions. It is also a way to involve parents in career guidance.

---

Profiling or portfolio arrangements seem to assume higher importance as the curriculum becomes more flexible, modular and individualised. They can be linked to the tutorial or homeroom systems that many countries, such as Denmark, the Netherlands, Korea and Spain have established.

*Parents, employers and others can make significant contributions.*

Alongside teachers, there is a strong case for more active involvement of parents, employers, former students and other community representatives in school career guidance programmes. Employers can be involved through the work experience and other experience-based schemes discussed above. Parents and former students can also be used in this way. A further reason for involving parents is to ensure that their influence on their children's career choices is well-informed, and supportive rather than controlling. Many such activities are organised on an ad hoc basis at the local level, but there are some examples of systematic programmes:

- In the United States, the Puente programme, created to help Latino students complete high school and become eligible for public colleges and universities in California, includes parent groups, partly to educate parents about college and its requirements, and partly to get parents to "let go" of their children. It also often takes parents on trips to local colleges (Grubb, 2002b).

- In Canada (New Brunswick), where many recipients of welfare support are single parents with adolescent children, workshops are being provided to help these parents understand career development issues and to assist them in supporting their teenagers as learners and workers. It is hoped that the workshops will also motivate and bring a sense of optimism to the parents themselves. The initiative represents a "family learning" approach to career development (Bezanson and Kellett, 2001).

- The Austrian National Union of Students has, for many years, provided a voluntary but highly organised programme of advisory services for final year (grade 12) school students to assist the transition to university life. This involves a comprehensive programme of visits to school classes to provide information on university study, as well as individual advice that is available to both prospective and current students in the offices of the Union. Those who take part in the school visits are provided with some training by the Union.

*These several ideas are embodied in the notion of a "guidance-oriented school"...*

These various approaches to schools' career education programmes have been brought together in Canada (Quebec) in the concept of the guidance-oriented school (Box 3.4). A similar approach can be seen in some schools in Luxembourg. This brings together a strong community partnership with a whole-school approach in which guidance is seen as being at the heart of the school's purpose.

*...and all have implications for school resources and management...*

All of these approaches to career guidance are broader than an approach based upon personal interviews. All have implications for the organisation of the school, and for the distribution of resources within the school. These implications go well beyond career guidance staff. As examples:

- Portfolio systems need to be allocated curriculum time for supported reflection, on a group and (preferably) individual basis.

Without such support, these systems can easily degenerate into mere paper systems, and their potential as career development processes can be lost.

- Programmes such as work experience, that require students to learn in the community, need appropriate insurance arrangements, and effective brokerage arrangements between enterprises and schools to ensure sufficient placements and assure their quality. Such arrangements need to be resourced.

- The involvement of teachers in guidance programmes, whether as career education teachers, or as supports for profiling and portfolio systems, or in tutorial or homeroom roles, has considerable implications both for initial teacher education and for ongoing staff development if programmes are to be of high quality.

---

### Box 3.4. **Guidance-oriented schools**

In Canada (Quebec), schools are being encouraged to develop the concept of the guidance-oriented school (*l'école orientante*). This is linked to wider competency-oriented school reforms. Personal and career planning is defined as one of five "broad areas of learning" throughout schooling. The aim is to provide support for students' identity development in primary school and guidance in career planning throughout secondary school. This is linked to ensuring that students understand the usefulness of their studies (in languages, mathematics, sciences and so on) and why they are studying them. To implement this concept, the number of qualified guidance specialists is being increased. In addition, the active involvement of all stakeholders is being promoted, first by encouraging discussion and collaboration between teachers and guidance staff, and then by developing partnerships with parents and the community. Schools are being permitted considerable flexibility in determining what a guidance-oriented school is within the broad parameters provided (ministère de l'Éducation Québec, 2001).

A similar approach, linking a broad concept of career guidance to wider school reform and to wider links between the school and its community, can be seen in how career guidance is being introduced into some Luxembourg *lycées*. There, the curriculum, which can be included in each of grades 7, 8 and 9, includes the transition from primary to secondary school, life and social skills, study methods and tutorial support in addition to career education. It teaches decision-making skills and career-management skills in addition to assisting students to make specific choices. Teachers deliver this curriculum, with support from school psychologists. Employers and parents are involved by, for example, explaining occupations to students. It includes work experience or job shadowing, mentoring by students in higher grades, and personal projects. Luxembourg has commissioned evaluations of these initiatives to assess the impact upon student progression and upon operation of the *lycées* (Centre de co-ordination des projets d'établissement, 2002).

---

***...as well as for the roles of career guidance staff.***

The whole-school approaches described above have considerable implications for the role of career guidance specialists within schools: an example is given in Box 3.5. They need to be viewed as consultants as well as direct service providers. This has significant implications for their training, which needs to include curriculum, consultancy and community liaison skills, as well as individual interviewing skills.

***These various elements must form a coherent programme.***

Whole-school approaches also have implications for school management. The contributions of guidance specialists, of teachers and of community resources need to be integrated into a coherent programme. This requires attention from the senior management of the school, and systematic planning. In Canada (Ontario), as an example, all school principals are required to develop a comprehensive written guidance and career education programme plan. In addition, they are required every three years to conduct a survey of students, parents, teachers and other partners to evaluate the delivery and effectiveness of all components of the programme.

---

### Box 3.5. **The changing roles of school guidance staff in Denmark**

In Denmark, as part of reforms in the vocational education and training system, some of the large technical colleges have recognised that the skills and concerns of the guidance counsellors are now at the heart of the teaching and learning process. They have accordingly sought to use their guidance counsellors not only for delivering services to students but also for working with teachers as consultants. This is replacing the guidance counsellors' own teaching commitments: it seems possible that in future the guidance counsellors will spend around half of their time on guidance work and the rest on consultancy work, and do no direct teaching apart from careers education.

---

## 3.2. Meeting needs of out-of-school and at-risk youth

*A major current policy concern is to reintegrate young drop-outs.*

In all OECD countries, attention has focused upon the problems associated with early school leaving as school completion rates have risen. This has involved the development of programmes for those early school leavers who are drifting in and out of unemployment, labour-market inactivity and marginal unskilled work. The aim is to support their reinsertion into formal learning, whether school-based or work-based. It has also involved the development of preventative programmes for those judged to be most at risk of leaving school early. Guidance is almost invariably a major element of both types of programme.

*Formal guidance agencies may be given responsibilities for this task...*

*Programmes targeted upon early school leavers*

Where there are formal guidance agencies with a continuing responsibility for young people, they are normally responsible for working with early school leavers. In Germany the Federal Employment Service continues to be accessible to young people who have left school. It operates a variety of pre-vocational programmes for young people who are experiencing difficulties in getting training places or a job. In England, the Connexions service is responsible for young people to the age of 19, whatever their educational status. It gives priority to those who are at risk as part of the government's policies to combat social exclusion.

*...or specific services may be set up for this purpose.*

Other countries have set up specific services for this group, and guidance is invariably part of what they do. In Denmark, municipalities are legally obliged to make contact with, and offer guidance to, young people who have dropped out of formal education on at least two occasions a year up to the age of 19. Some municipalities extend the system beyond this. In some cases this work is done by school guidance counsellors. In others, especially the larger municipalities, it is done by separate youth guidance counsellors. From the age of 18 such young people become entitled to limited income support, but only if they develop and implement action plans in consultation with the youth guidance service. The focus is on helping them to take up their rights to participate in education and training.

Very similar services exist in Norway and Sweden. In all three countries the combination of early intervention, mutual obligation and individual action planning appears to be very successful in reducing the number of young people under the age of 20 who are unemployed or not in the labour market (OECD, 2000a).

A similar, although less highly developed, model for early intervention at the local level to support early school leavers, and which also involves a strong guidance element, can be found in Luxembourg's *Action Locale pour Jeunes* service. It co-ordinates action for young people who are unemployed or otherwise in difficulty in the labour market. It systematically follows them up on an individual basis and tries to integrate them into employment. This help can take a variety of forms including individual guidance, the development of action plans, and training in job-seeking skills.

In Ireland, the Youthreach programme provides a safety net for early school leavers and unemployed youth. Programmes are located in a wide variety of settings: centres sponsored by local Vocational Education Committees; Community Training workshops that are funded by the Training and Employment Agency (FÁS); and Senior Traveller Training Centres. In the programme, the personal, social, educational and vocational problems experienced by many participants result in advice, guidance and counselling often forming part of the job of those who teach in the programme. Pilot programmes have been established to train them to do so. In addition, a guidance service is provided to each programme by qualified personnel on a limited part-time basis: these include staff from the Training and Employment Agency.

In Canada (Quebec), a network of non-profit *Carrefours Jeunesse-Emploi* (Youth Employment Centres) offer information and guidance alongside workshops and cultural, social and travel projects to young people aged 16-35, through a network of 106 service points. They focus particularly (though not exclusively) on young people at risk, and include outreach services to make contact with them.

*Such work needs to be highly individualised.*

Whatever the structure of such services, it seems that successful strategies involve a highly individualised approach, looking after young people's personal and social needs as well as their educational and vocational guidance needs. This can be done by career guidance staff working with youth workers, using outreach approaches. An alternative model, which is being trialled in England's Connexions service, is to have a single generic "first-in-line" role, supported by a range of specialists (including career guidance specialists) who can be brought in when needed.

It is much easier to reintegrate young people if they have a wide range of education and training programmes available to them, including ones that are specifically designed to meet their needs. The education system in Denmark includes options such as production schools (Moeller and Ljung, 1999) which let young people design their own curriculum rather than simply choosing between prescribed options. Guidance is strongly embedded in such structures.

*Preventive programmes in schools are also needed.*

*Programmes designed to prevent early school leaving*

Alongside reintegration services for young people who have already dropped out, there is a need for preventive programmes within schools. A strong career guidance involvement can also be observed in many of these types of programmes. As an example, in Luxembourg, the *Action Locale pour Jeunes* (ALJ) works closely with the *modulaire* classes of the *lycées techniques*, in which the weakest students, who are most likely to be at risk of unemployment, are concentrated. Teachers in these schools are given time to work with the ALJ. A further example of such a programme is presented in Box 3.6.

---

**Box 3.6. An Australian programme for working with at-risk students in schools**

The Jobs Pathways Programme (JPP) in Australia is managed by the federal Department of Education, Science and Training (DEST). It operates on a regional basis, with funding targeted particularly at regions with high levels of youth unemployment and low school completion rates.

JPP providers are awarded time-limited contracts based on competitive tendering. They include private for-profit organisations, private not-for-profit organisations, community organisations, schools and TAFE institutes. Their staff come from a variety of backgrounds, including teaching, youth work and social work; they are unlikely to have had any specific guidance training.

They service a number of schools, visiting periodically (perhaps once a week, perhaps every few weeks) to work mainly with at-risk about-to-leave students on an individual or group basis. In addition, young people who have left school but have not entered a course or full-time job can access JPP. Young people who have been receiving unemployment payments for six months may be referred to JPP providers as part of their "mutual obligation" requirements.

Participants receive an initial assessment to identify the help they need. This may include mentoring, preparation of resumes, interview preparation, job placement, and advocacy on their behalf. It may also include referral to a career counselling workshop and then working with the young person to implement the action plan arising from the workshop. Funding is based on the services provided rather than on outcomes.

---

## 3.3. Meeting needs in tertiary education

*Tertiary education has undergone major changes in OECD countries.*

Almost without exception, OECD countries have experienced very substantial increases in participation in tertiary education since the beginning of the 1990s. Between 1995 and 1999 alone, enrolment rates grew by an average of 23% across the OECD (OECD, 2001e). Expansion has been accompanied by change and diversification. The student body has become more diverse; new types of institutions with broader purposes than traditional universities have been created; attendance patterns have become more flexible; the courses offered have become wider; relationships with the community and the labour market have become closer in many cases and yet more diffuse in others; and competition between institutions has increased (OECD, 1997; OECD, 1998b; Grubb, 2003). All of these changes have created major challenges for career guidance.

*These changes pose major career guidance challenges...*

As institutions become more differentiated, as the number of institutions and courses to choose from increases, and as courses become more differentiated in content between institutions, the need grows for information and advice to help people decide what and where to study. As institutions become more competitive, the need for information and advice that is independent of the interests of particular institutions rises. Increased competition between institutions for students and for resources leads to the labour market outcomes of their graduates becoming a key marketing feature. It also leads institutions to become aware that their graduates' employability and career-management skills can be an important way for them to market themselves both to potential students and to employers. On all these grounds, the need for good quality consumer guides, reflecting the client perspective, grows stronger. As institutions and courses become more diverse, and as enrolments in courses that are not narrowly linked to specific professional qualifications grow, links between tertiary education and the labour market become more diffused and complex, increasing the need for more sophisticated ways to link graduates to post-graduation employment. Thus the need for career guidance services increases at the point of entry to tertiary education, during it, and at the interface between it and the labour market. This calls for a comprehensive approach.

*...which tertiary education is often ill-equipped to handle.*

Career guidance services in many countries' tertiary education systems are ill-equipped to handle these challenges. Commonly they are limited in scale, highly variable in their nature, and often address only some of the needs and challenges that they face. For example:

- In Australia, student outcomes surveys in technical and further education (TAFE) institutes have consistently shown student counselling services and career and job information to receive lower satisfaction ratings from graduates than any other aspects of their TAFE experience.

- In Austria, a survey has described services in higher education as "...a patchwork of services active at different institutions, in different geographical areas, with different forms of specialisations, that are not systematically organised so as to make all forms of guidance and counselling equally available to each student at each university" (Schilling and Moist, 1998).

- In Korea, it seems that 61% of students in four-year institutions have never received any on-campus career development services; even among those in their final two years, the figure is over 25%. Most services are one-off recruitment-oriented events such as special lectures or seminars. There is demand for better services both from students and from employers.

Most tertiary education institutions provide services to help students to study and choose courses (Watts and van Esbroeck, 1998). Such educational guidance services, however, usually pay little or no attention to career guidance, including the career implications of course choices. In almost all countries institutions are free to decide whether and how to provide career guidance.

*In most countries tertiary education guides are produced.*

In nearly all OECD countries, central tertiary education guides are produced to supplement the handbooks and promotional materials produced by individual institutions. Traditionally these have often been produced by Ministries of Education, and in print format, with final-year school students as the principal target group. Increasingly they are in electronic format. This can be in CD-ROM format, as in Ireland where high Internet access costs limit possibilities for on-line provision. It can also be on-line as in countries such as Australia, Finland, Korea and the United Kingdom. On-line guides have the advantage of being able to be updated quickly and cheaply. In some countries the private sector plays an active role in producing them, either under contract to governments as in Austria, Canada and the Netherlands or on a commercial basis as in Australia and the United Kingdom.

The distribution of such guides can be variable. In some countries they are distributed to all final-year (generally grade 12) school students. In other cases, for example in Austria, they are provided to school careers staff, but not directly to students.

*But these commonly contain quite limited information.*

Sometimes these central guides are comprehensive, providing information on the full range of tertiary study possibilities. However they are often segmented: providing information separately on courses in universities and in non-university institutions. Information on tertiary education can also be segmented on a regional basis. This is commonly the case in Spain, where the individual autonomous regions produce their own guides to tertiary study.

A major limitation of such guides in nearly all countries is that they are restricted to matters such as the content of courses and entry requirements. They rarely act as genuine consumer guides, as they do not contain information on matters such as student satisfaction with the quality of teaching and graduates' labour market outcomes. On the rare occasions that consumer guides are available to prospective students, as in Australia's Good Universities Guide (*www.thegoodguides.com.au*), they have generally been produced by the private sector rather than by central government agencies.

*Institutions vary in the extent to which they offer career guidance and in what they provide.*

The extent to which tertiary education institutions provide career guidance services varies considerably both between and within countries. Institutions usually have considerable freedom to decide what they offer. Four patterns can be distinguished:

- Counselling services. Career guidance is sometimes integrated into personal counselling services. Such services tend to have staff with counselling qualifications, but may have weak links with the labour market and concentrate mainly on personal problem counselling. In Austria, for example, the Federal

Ministry for Education, Science and Culture has established a network of six Psychological Student Counselling Centres to deal with personal, emotional and study problems, but careers services are relatively under-developed.

- Integrated student services. Some institutions have an integrated student services model which includes career guidance among a range of other student welfare services.

- Placement services. These focus mainly on job placement. They may include on-campus recruitment services. In addition to post-graduation jobs, they may include placement into vacation jobs and part-time jobs. Such services may offer limited attention to students' career development. This is the case for example in Korea where separate placement services and counselling services tend to be the principal forms of student services available.

- Specialised careers services. Some institutions have separate careers services which offer a variety of career guidance and placement services. Separate specialised careers services are well established in Ireland and the United Kingdom, and to a lesser extent in Australia, and are growing in some other European countries, including Finland, Germany, the Netherlands and Norway. Box 3.7 provides an example of a specialised careers service. In Germany, students also have access to the Federal Employment Service's higher education teams, which are based in institutions that have more than 10 000 students.

*Some institutions are introducing career education programmes.*

There is growing recognition in some countries of the need for tertiary institutions to develop employability and career-management skills in their students. Career-management courses have been developed in a number of institutions, particularly in Australia, Canada, Korea and the United Kingdom, and also in Spain. In many cases these lead to credits, and in a few institutions they are mandatory. They may include opportunities for work experience in the form of co-operative education programmes, internships, work shadowing or work simulation. They may include profiling and portfolio systems. In Australia and the United Kingdom, and to some extent in Germany, a number of universities have introduced portfolio systems. These can require students to record not only what they are learning, but also the work-related competencies they are acquiring through learning it.

*Performance contracts can be a direct way for governments to influence tertiary education careers services.*

The traditional autonomy of tertiary institutions limits the scope for central governments to directly shape and influence career guidance services. In the United Kingdom a major review of university careers services (Harris, 2001) has helped to focus debate within universities upon career guidance, and has generated interest within some institutions in change and reform, even if the scope for direct government intervention to improve services is relatively limited. Performance contracts are a more direct mechanism for influencing tertiary education careers services. These are widely used by governments in many OECD countries for monitoring and controlling performance, quality and funding in tertiary education (OECD, 2003d). Finland offers an example of the use of such an instrument to influence career guidance in tertiary education. There, a review of tertiary careers services highlighted considerable variation in the level and quality of provision. This has resulted in new requirements for the annual financial contract between universities and the Ministry of Education to include a concrete plan to improve guidance services, and for strategies to promote guidance within new study programmes.

---

### Box 3.7. **A specialised tertiary careers service**

The Careers Advisory Service at Trinity College Dublin (*www.tcd.ie/Careers/*) provides a wide range of services to students, graduates, academic staff and employers.

In addition to personal advice, **students** have access to a comprehensive careers library and to a range of on-line resource materials. The Service organises careers days that enable students to make contact with employers to discuss post-graduation employment. It provides students with access to job vacancies, and helps to arrange internships, work experience and vacation employment. Regular seminars are held throughout the year on job seeking skills, including video rehearsal of interview skills. Students can have access to psychological testing to assist their career decision-making. The Service arranges opportunities for students to be mentored by recent young graduates for short periods in order to better prepare themselves for post-graduation employment. A personal development programme is run within eight of the university's departments to help develop employability skills.

**Graduates** of Trinity College are able to use the Service for personal advice, for help with job placement, and to use the careers library.

**Employers** are provided with access to students for recruitment purposes, and can post vacancies with the Service. A range of company directories are available in the Service, employers are regularly surveyed on the qualities that they require in graduates, and graduates are surveyed annually to determine where they are working.

There are **academic staff** in each school or department responsible for liaising with the Careers Advisory Service. The Service works actively with academic staff to ensure that they refer students appropriately to the service, and academic staff have a close involvement with the personal development programme, which forms a formal part of the academic curriculum.

---

## CHAPTER 4. MEETING THE CAREER GUIDANCE NEEDS OF ADULTS

This chapter describes the main settings in which career guidance is provided to adults in OECD countries, sets out some of the specific issues that arise in these settings, and suggests some options for filling some of the more important gaps in career guidance for adults.

The chapter's key policy conclusions are that:

♦ The focus of public employment services upon the unemployed limits their capacity to provide career guidance that can address longer-term career development needs, or provide career guidance to those who are employed.

♦ Career guidance services in adult education can be too closely tied to the self-interest of particular educational institutions. Regionally-based independent services are one solution to this problem. Systematic feedback from career guidance services can help to improve the match between the supply of adult learning and the demand for it.

♦ Community-based career guidance services for adults can be more accessible and closer to the needs of particular target groups. On the other hand they can be more variable in quality and fragmented in their approach.

♦ A number of approaches can be used to influence the provision of career guidance within the workplace. These include linking it to training levies, quality-mark schemes that reward firms with good human resource development practices, and services delivered through trade unions.

♦ The chapter suggests two approaches to addressing some of the gaps in the provision of career guidance for adults. These include a wider role for public employment services, and wider use of regionally-based partnerships. Other strategies for increasing adults' access to career guidance are suggested in the following chapters.

## 4.1. Public employment services

*Much provision for adults is in public employment services...*

Traditionally, career guidance services for adults have been largely concentrated in public employment services. The major users of such services have been the unemployed, as well as other groups on the edge of the labour market such as disabled people.

*...and addresses short-term objectives...*

Services for such groups tend to focus on getting them a job as quickly as possible in order to reduce unemployment levels and income-security payments (and, in cases where there are concerns about overall labour shortages, to increase labour force participation rates). Sometimes help with job placement is offered on a self-service basis. Sometimes training is required before people can be placed in jobs. This can be in job-seeking skills, in basic skills, or in specific vocational skills. Training is frequently preceded by some employment counselling, partly to advise people, but also to decide how much training the state is prepared to provide. This commonly leads to a case-managed action plan which is required in order to maintain eligibility for income support. In other words, the counselling often performs gatekeeping and policing functions in relation to public resources. It is not just to help the individual make decisions, but also to make institutional decisions about the individual.

*...requiring gatekeeping and benefit-policing as well as guidance roles.*

For example in Denmark, unemployed adults are only allowed to remain on benefits for five years, and before the end of 12 months of unemployment (six months in the case of individuals under the age of 25) they must be activated. This involves them seeing a placement officer or guidance counsellor and developing an individual action plan. This plan can include gaining entry into education and training, a job, or a job-creation programme. The fact that the guidance is linked to the administration of benefit entitlements may place some limits on its neutrality. In Germany, unemployed people are obliged to attend placement and guidance services in order to maintain their rights to benefits.

*This can lead to role conflict.*

Where the administrative and counselling tasks are combined there can be some role conflict. For example the longer-term interests of the individual may require a higher investment in training than is necessary for short-term job entry. More generally, counselling requires people to be open and honest, and the gatekeeping and benefit-policing tasks are likely to restrict this. Administrative tasks may also consume much of the time that might be available for counselling. Such role conflicts might be unavoidable in the interests of efficient administration of public employment services. Rather than an argument for resolving them, they might point to the need for additional sources of impartial career guidance that can be accessed by the unemployed.

*Despite this, the trend in some countries has been towards integration of such roles...*

In some countries, the trend in recent years has been to integrate rather than separate such roles, and to weaken career guidance structures in public employment services. In Denmark, for example, the roles of guidance counsellor and placement officer have recently become more blurred. Placement officers may offer some basic guidance, and guidance counsellors may be involved in developing individual action plans.

Previously the guidance counsellors sat to some extent outside the organisational culture. Now, however, they are more integrated into it. It is a culture which is strongly focused on serving the needs of the labour market and on leading to a concrete outcome: entry to employment or education and training. The training for the guidance counsellor role is conducted in-house, as part of the general training programme for public employment service staff. It comprises a two-week course on top of the basic three-month initial training. This is a reduction from the former training pattern. It seems, then, that the role of the guidance counsellor within the service has changed to some extent from a client-centred role to an organisational role.

In Norway, the public employment service used to offer career guidance to schools and to others. The Employment Act still formally requires it to "provide vocational guidance to those who need it". But with the rise in unemployment the service to schools was withdrawn in the mid-1980s, and since then career guidance has almost entirely disappeared as a separate service. Instead it is part of the general placement services. In the new in-house web-based staff training programme, career guidance has proved to be one of the most popular options; the training is however fairly basic in nature, and the opportunities for staff to use such skills are limited.

In Canada, screening interviews and case management have in some cases been contracted out to third-party organisations, which are not eligible for the training provided to employment counsellors by the federal government.

*...within an administrative culture.*

Often, the main training provided for employment service staff is administrative rather than guidance training. In Luxembourg, for example, the staff of the ADEM-OP (*Administration d'Emploi-Orientation Professionelle*) are generally recruited under normal civil service conditions, and are not required to have specific career guidance qualifications. Even in Germany, where career guidance constitutes a separate occupational category within the public employment service, with its own separate training arrangements, only around one in five of those in career counsellor roles within the Federal Employment Service have been trained on the three-year undergraduate courses at the Service's own *Fachhochschule* in Mannheim. Most of the rest have been on generic three-year courses in public administration in the *Fachhochschule* and then after work experience in the Federal Employment Service have undertaken relatively short six-month courses in career counselling. This means that their training as counsellors is more limited, and that they tend to approach it within an administrative mind-set.

On the other hand, as indicated in Chapter 1, Finland has retained a separate career guidance service within its public employment service. Elsewhere, too, there are signs of moves towards a separate and more highly trained workforce. In Australia, a Career Counselling Programme has been established by the federal government and its delivery is contracted out. The programme is available to young people aged 15-20 who are registered as job-seekers but are not eligible for income support. It is also available to job-seekers of all ages who are receiving activity-tested income support. Participants receive career counselling in groups and in some cases may receive individual sessions. The programme is distinctive because it has set strong standards for staff: the career counsellors involved must have an appropriate tertiary qualification (preferably at postgraduate level) in career guidance or counselling, must be able to demonstrate at least five years' recent experience in providing career counselling to young people, and must be affiliated to a state or national career counselling organisation.

In Ireland, nearly eight in ten of the employment service staff who provide career guidance have had at least some form of guidance training. They can undertake a part-time university course in adult guidance over a twelve-month period, with their tuition fees and release time for course attendance being paid for, and with salary increments for those who successfully complete the course. A goal has been set for increasing the number of staff who have such qualifications. In Korea, where current training for employment service staff is limited, there are plans to move towards a structure of bachelor and master's degrees, possibly linked to training for human resource staff and industrial trainers. A few universities are developing courses of this kind, but as yet they have no official status.

*There is a trend towards one-stop centres.*

In several countries, there has been a trend towards establishing one-stop centres: co-locating employment and welfare services, so that welfare clients can more readily access the range of services they need:

- In Australia, the first port-of-call for job-seekers is Centrelink, which offers information about education, training and employment assistance, and administers a variety of welfare benefits. It then refers those who are eligible to other employment services. Thus it operates both as a one-stop portal and as a filtering mechanism.

- In the Netherlands, 131 Centres for Work and Income have been established across the country, to provide initial one-stop centres for both job-information and benefit-claimant services. Staff come from a mix of employment and social-security backgrounds: the aim is to merge the two roles, mainly through in-house training.

- In England and Northern Ireland a merger of the Employment Service and the Benefits Agency has resulted in the creation of Jobcentre Plus to provide an integrated approach to the reduction of welfare dependency.

- A similar trend exists in Canada, and moves in the same direction are under consideration in Norway. One-stop centres are common, too, in the United States (Bezanson and Kellett, 2001).

*Services for employed people are often web-based and impersonal; personal services for them are usually limited.*

Most public employment services offer web-based career guidance to those who are employed. For example:

- In Korea, the Work-Net web site provides individuals with access to job vacancies, and employers with access to job seekers. It contains a wide range of occupational and labour market information and data on training courses. In addition, it offers on-line test administration and on-line information-oriented counselling services. WorkNet is widely used by employed people who are thinking of changing jobs as well as by the unemployed.

- In the Netherlands, a new web site has been developed (www.werk.nl/) which includes diagnostic instruments (based on interests), data on occupations (including labour-market trends and salary data), information on education and training opportunities, and access to a web version of the database of job vacancies. There are also plans to develop a client-support centre, to be accessible by telephone, e-mail, fax and post.

- In Norway, the public employment service (Aetat) has developed a range of self-help tools, many of them web-based. These include: an interest inventory; a career choice programme which offers self-assessments of interests, work values and skills, plus an occupational matching facility and help with job-seeking (Veivalg); and a career learning programme (Gradplus) adapted from the United Kingdom and addressed mainly to higher education graduates. There are proposals under consideration to set up a call centre to respond to enquiries about learning and work.

Web-based services are either not accessible to or do not meet the needs of all adults. Other career guidance services available within public employment services to employed clients are usually limited, and offered largely on a self-service basis. For example in Norway, access to the service's web site is provided on a walk-in basis, along with printed vacancy information, word-processing facilities for writing job applications and curricula vitae, free telephones for contacting employers, and some limited staff support. In Canada, public employment offices across the country include resource centres which have Internet access and paper-based materials. In general, however, these have limited space, and staff support for such resources is usually confined to administrative help (for print-outs, booking machines, etc.) rather than skilled information support.

Even where the services are more extensive, their image tends to restrict their use. In Denmark, as an example, the guidance counsellors and placement officers in the public employment service are in principle available to everyone; in practice, however, the stigma stemming from their association with the unemployed deters many other people from using them.

*Some countries have redesigned their centres to attract more employed people.*

A few countries have been attempting to attract more employed people by redesigning their centres to give less prominence to queues for welfare payments. In the Netherlands, in marketing the new Centres for Work and Income, greater emphasis is being placed on the employed group than on the unemployed. Benefit claimant services are kept to the back end of the centres. An electronic vacancy databank using a touch-screen approach includes not only directly notified vacancies but also other vacancies taken from press advertisements. Other career information resources include free web and telephone access. Staff are available to provide brief personal help where it is needed. Similarly, in Norway, the public employment service's centres are being redesigned to include state-of-the-art amenities that are attractive and accessible: welfare-claimant services operate discreetly behind screens at the back. In general, however, the effectiveness of public employment services continues to be measured largely by how fast they return benefit claimants to work, rather than by broader criteria.

*Career guidance services may exist for groups such as immigrants and prisoners.*

### Other public services

Other public career guidance services may be offered to particular target-groups. These may include immigrants, asylum seekers and offenders. In Canada, there are special employment services for immigrants, funded by Citizenship and Immigration Canada and by some of the provinces as part of their settlement and adaptation programmes. These services include employment counselling, job-search programmes, help with recognition of foreign credentials, and prior learning assessment. In Ireland, career guidance is provided by the Training and Employment Agency's Asylum Seekers Unit. It is also provided within prisons, normally as part of pre-release programmes. Services provided by trained guidance counsellors are complemented by less structured guidance provided by probation officers, chaplains, teachers in the prison education service and the like.

## 4.2. Services within adult education

*Adults enrolled in education have access to their institution's career guidance services.*

Some countries such as Austria, Denmark and Spain have developed guidance services within adult education. Enrolled adults have access to the career guidance services available to all students. Some such services pay more attention than others to the needs of mature students, including the rather different position they may have in relation to the labour market. Many of these services are stronger on educational opportunities than on labour-market issues, and tend to focus mainly on the institution in which they are based. This may limit their comprehensiveness and impartiality.

*Some institutions have extended career guidance services to adults in the community.*

Some tertiary education institutions offer guidance services to adults who are not enrolled. They do this in three different ways:

- As part of strategies to build relationships with alumni, which might lead in due course to alumni bequests and other benefits. Such strategies are common in the United States, and are beginning to develop in countries such as Australia, Canada and the United Kingdom.

- As part of access strategies designed to lead to possible enrolments.

- As fee-paying services. Some universities offer such services in Australia and the United Kingdom.

In some cases there may be a mix of these strategies. For example in Technical and Further Education (TAFE) institutes in Australia (New South Wales), people who are not sure whether they will study in TAFE are entitled to one free visit at which it is determined whether they are likely to be a TAFE student. If so, they are offered career counselling; if not, they are offered information and referred elsewhere (usually to private services) or offered career counselling for a fee.

*Guidance may also be included in access courses…*

Some institutions run access courses, sometimes in community centres, for adults returning to formal learning after a substantial gap. These often include strong guidance elements, designed to help such adults not only to develop their study skills but also to determine what and why they want to learn.

*…and in processes for assessment and recognition of prior learning.*

A growing trend in countries such as Canada, the Netherlands and Norway is the introduction of processes for the assessment and recognition of prior learning, including learning which has been acquired informally. Such processes can be only a technical procedure, assessing whether people can enter a given programme or meet the requirements of a specific qualification. Alternatively, they can also develop into a guidance dialogue, in which people are helped to identify and value the knowledge and competencies they have acquired informally, and to explore new opportunities to which they might be transferable.

*It can also play an important role in the informal adult and community education sector.*

Career guidance can be provided in the more informal adult and community education sector, which is often a significant provider of second-chance opportunities for adults. In Australia, the Full Steam Ahead programme in the Australian Capital Territory helps adult learners to focus on what they want in life and encourages them to explore their beliefs and values and to identify and overcome barriers. In Victoria the Learning Town programme has set up a careers library in eight community-based adult education providers and organised career guidance training for a member of staff from each provider. In Ireland, a number of pilot adult education guidance programmes have been established, designed to provide support to adults who are enrolled in literacy, community education and other programmes.

*Ensuring that career guidance is impartial is a key issue.*

A key issue in providing career guidance for potential adult education students is to ensure that it is impartial, and does not inadvertently or openly promote the interests of particular institutions through attempting to recruit students or failing to refer them to alternative sources of learning. One approach to this, on a large scale, is the regional adult information, advice and guidance partnerships that have been created throughout

England, and the related regionally-based guidance services that provide assistance to adults in Scotland and Wales.[1] The partnerships in England have been created as a part of the government's strategy to encourage poorly qualified and low-skilled adults to return to education (Department for Education and Employment, 1998). These services must account for their performance by reporting the numbers from key target groups such as single parents and ex-offenders that have been assisted. An example of a similar pilot programme on a smaller scale in Austria is given in Box 4.1. The example in Box 4.1 also illustrates how career guidance services can be used in adult education to provide systematic feedback on adults' learning needs, thus improving the match between the supply of learning and the demand for it.

---

Box 4.1. **A regionally-based adult education guidance service**

In the county of Burgenland the Austrian Ministry of Education has established a regional service to provide career guidance that is independent of particular adult education providers. The service is located in a regional adult education support centre, rather than in an institution that provides adult education. It has a high proportion of women who are unemployed or seeking to return to work among its clients. It sees adult education providers as its clients, as well as individuals. Its services are free. In order to give information and guidance to people where they are located and at times that are convenient to them, it provides guidance by telephone and by e-mail as well as face-to-face. It provides guidance to smaller communities in the region on a peripatetic basis, rather than requiring all clients to travel to the regional centre. It is committed to using data to improve its client services. It was established in conjunction with a survey to define client needs, it maintains a computerised database of client needs and problems and feeds results from this to adult education providers, and it is being evaluated in association with the University of Graz. It makes intelligent use of the local media in order to publicise its services and to increase access. It communicates with regional adult education providers through a regular newsletter, and has developed a database of adult education advisors in the region to help it keep in touch with regional institutions.

---

## 4.3.     Community-based services

*Career guidance may be offered by community-based organisations.*

A recent development in a number of countries has been the growth of career guidance services in community-based organisations. Some of these focus on particular ethnic groups; some on groups such as single parents, people with particular disabilities, ex-offenders, or the homeless.

*Some countries have deliberately enhanced such provision.*

In Australia and Canada the growth of such services has been stimulated by the contracting-out of some public employment services to these kinds of organisations. (Chapter 8 discusses the issue of contracting out in more detail.) Part of the rationale for such contracting out is that the organisations concerned are often perceived by members of their target-groups as being more accessible and more attuned to their needs. The result of such policies can be the creation of a major sector of guidance provision (see Box 4.2).

---

1.      These arrangements are complemented by a national telephone help line (learndirect) which is mentioned in Chapter 1 and described in more detail in Chapter 5.

---

### Box 4.2. **Community-based services in Canada**

In Canada, it is estimated that there are probably over 10 000 community-based organisations delivering career development services. Many are small, with perhaps 5-7 full-time-equivalent staff; though some are much larger, with as many as 100 or 200 employees over a variety of locations. Some of these organisations focus on career development activities such as information services, career guidance and job-search workshops. Many have a wider range of functions, including various forms of education and training and community work. Some of these, such as literacy programmes, may include career development elements. This may enable them to adopt more holistic approaches to the needs of their clients.

Often their funds come from a range of different government sources. In many cases a lot of their funding is project-based. This can lead to staff turnover and risk their continued survival. The community-based sector in Canada is generally fragmented, under-resourced and has limited access to support structures. Some services employ trained career guidance staff but many do not. To address these issues, the federal government has supported a range of networks, mainly at provincial level.

A notable such national initiative is Career Circuit. It supports community-based organisations offering career development services to young people, especially those who have left school. It is based on a partnership created by the government between three non-profit organisations: the Canadian Career Development Foundation, the Canadian Foundation for Economic Education and the Canadian Youth Foundation. It offers on-line networking between over 5 000 agencies, a searchable database of career resources, and a self-instructional training programme, supported by a network of trainers. A number of Regional Representatives, with a mix of career development and other qualifications plus community development experience, have been employed to liaise between and support the agencies.

---

*It can take varied forms.*

Community-based services can take many forms. In Korea, there are around a hundred women's centres, some funded by the national government and some by the provinces. In addition to providing social centres, they may run education and training courses, and offer career information and counselling services (see Box 4.3). In Luxembourg, local action projects run by voluntary and not-for-profit organisations include the Full Employment Network (*Reseau Objectif Plein Emploi*), a programme for women who are victims of domestic violence (the *Femmes en détresse* project) and local and regional development projects. Such projects are financed from a range of sources; generally their staff do not have specific training in guidance and their roles include a wide range of other functions.

*Community-based provision potentially has both strengths and weaknesses.*

The merits of policy strategies that work through community-based organisations include not only their greater knowledge of, and acceptability to, particular client groups, but also the contribution they can make to community capacity building (Bezanson and Kellett, 2001). Some accordingly hold the view that they should be used as the conduit for most public services, including those in the guidance field. On the other hand, others take the view that this sector is fragmented, idiosyncratic, and sometimes anti-government and anti-bureaucratic, and that it too often consumes public funds without discernible outcomes (see Grubb, 2002b). It seems likely that the sector has a contribution to make to career guidance strategies for adults, but alongside – rather than as a substitute for – more formal services.

---

Box 4.3. **A women's development centre in Korea**

Kyonggi Women's Development Centre is widely viewed in Korea as a "beacon centre" in terms of its information and counselling services.

Alongside its training courses, it helps women who want to set up their own business (including "incubator" facilities), and runs one-week career planning courses for unemployed women and for single mothers. It provides web-based and face-to-face career guidance services which include testing programmes and a job-placement service. Its web-based services include databases on educational courses, child-care facilities, women experts, and companies with women as chief executives. It was built by women employed through a public-works programme.

Among the staff of the centre are several people with social-welfare and counselling qualifications.

---

## 4.4. Employment-based services[2]

*Many employees look to their employer for career guidance, and some employers provide it.*

Many employed people look to their employer for career guidance, both on learning new skills and on career development within the organisation (MORI, 2001). Some employers offer systematic career guidance to their staff. This tends to be confined to larger enterprises and, with some exceptions, to managerial and professional staff:

- In Australia, the Queensland Police Service offers help with career-planning to all staff, including low-skilled staff. This includes access to career planning officers, mentors, workbooks, workshops, and a web site containing skill profiles of all the main positions within the organisation.

- In the Netherlands, a few large employers have established mobility centres for their employees. These centres are often staffed by human resource development specialists, supported by external consultants. These may provide training needs assessments. The centres are concerned mainly with internal movement within the company, but may also let employees explore opportunities in the external labour market, depending on whether the company is prepared to support this or not.

*Governments have used training levies to encourage firms to provide career guidance...*

In some countries, governments have encouraged such provision, in two ways. The first is by including career guidance as allowable expenditure against training levies:

- In Canada (Quebec), there is a legal stipulation that employers must demonstrate that they spend one per cent of their payroll on employee training, which may include career development services leading to training plans.

---

2.     In addition to the services provided by employers and trade unions that are discussed here, a range of career guidance services exist that can be purchased on the market in the private sector. These are normally provided by private consultants, management consultancy firms, outplacement firms and the like. They are discussed in Chapter 8.

- In the Netherlands, some sectors of employment, in total covering around 38% of all employees, have developed their own training schemes, based on training levy funds from employers and employees. These are particularly important for small- and medium-sized organisations, which often lack their own training arrangements. The schemes may include access to some limited sector-specific career guidance from training officers.

- In Korea, companies with over 1 000 employees must invest at least two per cent of their payroll in training. If they do not, they pay the balance as a training levy. There is little evidence of companies establishing career development reviews to support such training programmes, but the potential is there.

*...and quality-mark schemes.*

The second is through voluntary quality-mark schemes. In the Netherlands and the United Kingdom, a government-subsidised Investors in People programme provides a quality-mark to companies that adopt good human resource development practices. In the Netherlands, this includes encouragement for companies to use careers advisers to support their development review systems.

**Career guidance is commonly part of outplacement packages.**

Many employers include career guidance services in outplacement packages when they decide to dismiss staff. Such services are usually purchased from outside providers. Sometimes, in the case of mass redundancies, governments may provide some financial support for such schemes. This happens, for example, in Canada.

**Some trade unions provide career guidance to their members.**

In some countries, trade unions are playing an increasing role in employment-based career guidance. They are doing so by negotiating for it within collective bargaining, and as career guidance providers in their own right. A major advantage of such schemes is that low-qualified and low-skilled workers may be more likely to informally approach a union representative in the workplace than to make an appointment at an external career guidance centre staffed by fully-qualified practitioners.

- In Denmark, Norway and the United Kingdom, some unions have run courses to train their shop stewards to act as "educational ambassadors" or "learning representatives" in encouraging their members (especially those with limited or no qualifications) to access education and training. This programme is extensive in the United Kingdom and receives strong support both from government and from the trade union movement (*www.learningservices.org.uk/*). In late 2002 there were around 3 500 Union Learning Representatives in the United Kingdom, and their number is projected to increase to perhaps seven times this by 2010 (Cabinet Office, 2002). The Employment Act 2002 has given Union Learning Representatives a statutory right to carry out their duties, and to be adequately trained.

- Some trade unions provide direct career guidance for their members in Canada, the Netherlands and Spain. In Austria both employer organisations and the trade unions provide direct career guidance. The trade unions, through the Chamber of Labour, tend to concentrate upon career guidance for the unemployed. Personal career guidance provided by the employers' Economic Chambers is provided on a fee-paying basis, although at a subsidised cost. In addition, the Economic Chambers provide extensive career information centres.

*Many employer-based services are limited in their impartiality and comprehensiveness.*

A potential limitation of career guidance services provided by employers is that there may be a conflict of interest between the employer and the employee. If for example an employer wants to retain an employee, he/she may not be willing to support access to guidance services which encourage the person to investigate jobs in other organisations.

## 4.5.    Filling gaps in provision

*There are major gaps in current provision for adults.*

Despite the diversity of career guidance services available to adults, major gaps exist in all countries. One gap is services for employed adults, especially those in small- and medium-sized organisations. Another is for people who have been outside the labour market for a while and are not entitled to employment services or to social assistance: for example women returning to the labour market and refugees. There may be other gaps: for example, workers displaced by employers who do not provide outplacement services. In addition many services for adults are quite narrowly targeted: for example on particular educational institutions, or their own workplace.

*These include career guidance for older age groups.*

A gap that is evident in many countries is the limited scope of career guidance for older workers and for the "third age". In the United Kingdom, recent reviews of guidance for the third age have revealed a wide range of disconnected provision (Ford, 1997; Department for Education and Skills, 2003). Many countries are concerned about their ageing population and the problems this is increasingly posing for increased health and old age security expenditure. To relieve the pressures on public resources, policies are being developed to maintain employment among older workers and promote their re-entry into the labour market. This can be linked to encouraging more flexible approaches to managing the transition to retirement. It can also be linked to encouraging those who have left the labour market to continue their involvement in learning and in voluntary work in the community, so reducing health bills and harnessing their social contribution (OECD, 1998b; OECD, 2000b). Policy responses to ageing societies in most OECD countries have, to date, largely focused upon reforms to retirement age provision and reformed income support arrangements. There are strong arguments for public policy seeking stronger links between these reforms and the availability of career guidance to help people to create more flexible transitions to retirement. In particular, a much closer integration between financial planning and career guidance, as part of overall retirement planning, could assist people to put together more flexible mixes of temporary employment, part-time work, and self-employment during the transition to retirement.

As yet, no country has developed a systematic approach to career guidance for the third age. Some provision exists in a few countries:

- In Australia (Western Australia), the Profit from Experience Programme, funded by the state's Department of Training and accessed through community-based Joblinks, supports mature-age people to re-enter the workforce.

- In Korea, 36 "manpower banks" for older workers have been set up in a variety of organisations including the YMCA, Korean Elderly Association centres and social welfare centres.

*There is evidence of unmet demand.*

In a number of countries, there are strong indications that demand for career guidance by adults exceeds the supply of services. For example:

- Where openly accessible services exist, they are heavily used, often leading to queues and bottlenecks (this is the case, for example, with the career counselling services in the public employment services in Finland and Germany).

- Many services take care to limit their publicity for fear of being overrun. In Canada (Manitoba), for instance, employment counselling is freely available in principle but is not widely publicised for fear that the ensuing demand might exceed supply. For similar reasons the already stretched career guidance service in Finland's public employment service does not actively advertise itself.

- Some services designed for young people are regularly approached by adults. This can be observed in Australia, where 60% of the clients of a small national network of Career Information Centres designed for young people are adults, and in Norway. In Austria, the career information centres (BIZ) of the Federal Employment Office were initially designed as a service largely for youth. However adults now constitute 47% of their clients, and in 2001 the number of adult users grew by 15%.

It also seems likely that much potential demand is untapped. In the United Kingdom, a national telephone guidance and information service for adults was launched in February 1998, accompanied by extensive media marketing. By the end of 2000, it had received 2.4 million calls (Watts and Dent, 2002) and over five million by mid 2003.

A level of demand that exceeds supply is unsurprising, given that most career guidance services are free. A common solution to such situations is to seek to ration supply: for example by setting priorities for the provision of services; or allowing the imposition of a price to ration services. However such solutions might not be compatible with a goal of seeking to expand access to career guidance, for all who wish it, throughout the lifespan. These issues are taken up further in the discussion of market-based approaches in Chapter 8.

*Open-access career centres for all adults are limited.*

Few countries currently have open-access career centres, available to all adults. Even where they exist, they tend to be limited in number and restricted in the range of services they offer. In Australia for example there are only 12 Career Information Centres that are open to the general public. In Denmark, there have been a few experiments in setting up open-access career centres in well-populated locations, but some have closed after a period because there has been no framework for sustaining them.

*There are a number of ways to fill these gaps.*

Options available to policy-makers to widen adult access to career guidance include the adoption of more innovative approaches to service delivery – based, for example around ICT and telephone technology – and the stimulation of private markets for career guidance, including through adopting innovative approaches to financing career guidance. The first of these is discussed in Chapter 5. Chapter 8 discusses the role of private markets in career guidance.

*One strategy is to expand the role of public employment services...*

Another strategy would be to consider a wider role for public employment services than their current focus on short-term goals with restricted target-groups (OECD, 2001c) so that their role is more closely integrated into national lifelong learning strategies: encompassing an added emphasis upon sustaining employability (Bouquin, 2001). The adoption of such an approach would involve expanding public employment centres to include career development centres, building on their current information resource centres but making these more central. It would involve redesigning the centres to appeal to a wider clientele, with a clearer physical separation between career development and benefit-claimant services. The existing emphasis in many public employment services' career information centres on providing information on learning and work opportunities would need to be expanded to make the available information more comprehensive, and to ensure the availability of appropriately trained and qualified staff to help provide information and to give personal advice. It would also require the adoption of clear branding and marketing strategies to promote the service and aid public recognition.

*...possibly drawing upon the strengths of current services in Germany and Norway.*

Drawing from existing practice, a model might be provided by bringing together the respective strengths of two systems:

- The career information centres (BIZ) in Germany. These are available at almost every local employment office. They include a variety of information on occupations in printed and videodisc form, as well as audiotapes on questions relating to university studies, and access to electronic databases. Administrative and information staff are available to provide brief help; some centres also make a career counsellor available. Similar centres exist in both Austria and Luxembourg, although not necessarily in every public employment centre.

- The innovative features of the public employment service in Norway (Aetat), including the design-quality of its new walk-in services, the quality of its web site (with its user-friendly and comprehensive vacancy listings), its inventive range of web-based tools, and its plans to set up a call centre for information on learning and work.

*The implications of such a strategy would need to be carefully considered.*

Such a strategy would have many implications, and would need careful consideration in light of current demands and pressures upon public employment services. Specific considerations include:

- implications for the costs of public employment services;

- implications for the obligation of public employment services to ensure that the unemployed are able and willing to quickly return to work;

- whether an expanded role should include access to in-depth assessment and personal advice, as it does in Denmark, Finland and Germany. If so whether this should be free or charged for; whether it should be available only to certain target groups; or whether it should be available by referral to other agencies; and

- implications for staffing, including their recruitment, qualifications and training.

*Another strategy is to form local partnerships between existing providers...*

Another strategy for addressing current gaps in adult access to career guidance might be to form local partnerships between existing providers such as employment services, universities, colleges, adult education centres, community-based agencies, employers, unions and private-sector agencies. Potentially, such an approach can involve:

- clear and mutually agreed quality standards;

- better information being available to people about the full range of local services.

- clear referral mechanisms that recognise the strengths and weaknesses of the different sources of career guidance.

- local strategies to fill local gaps (Bezanson and Kellet, 2001).

There are a number of examples that can be drawn upon:

- Human Resources Development Canada (HRDC) has published a Partnership Handbook for use by its regional and local offices, designed to encourage a co-operative rather than competitive culture in relation to the contracting out of employment services. In Toronto, a partnership has been formed between the HRDC employment offices and a number of community agencies, aimed at providing seamless services to clients.

- In England, as outlined in Section 4.2, funding has been provided to enable career guidance partnerships for adults to be formed at local level in all areas of the country, with clear target groups of low-qualified and low-skilled adults. In Scotland and Wales, similar regionally-based services have been established, but with charters to provide services to youth as well as adults.

- In Denmark, there are 14 Regional Guidance Committees (VFU), linked to the structure of Regional Labour Market Councils. All the major guidance services are represented on the VFUs, with a secretariat provided by the public employment service. Their role includes distributing information and running staff-development. They commonly have sub-committees dealing with the key interfaces: between youth education and higher education, for example, or between different services for adults. They also co-ordinate a structure of local guidance committees, which conduct similar activities at local level.

*...with different levels of co-operation.*

Such partnerships might work at a number of levels. These include:

- Communication: where no working patterns are changed, but efforts are made to help services to understand what each other offers so that they can, for example, cross-refer clients appropriately.

- Co-operation: where two or more services co-operate on some joint task.

- Co-ordination: where two or more services alter their working patterns to bring them more closely into line with one another, while remaining within their existing boundaries.

- Cross-fertilisation: where efforts are made to encourage services to share and exchange skills, and in effect to work across boundaries in ways that are likely to redraw the boundaries themselves.

- Integration: where the cross-fertilisation process is developed to a point which means that the boundaries between the different services disappear altogether (Watts, Guichard, Plant and Rodriguez, 1994).

*Such partnerships could be networked and supported nationally.*

National policy can support partnership arrangements in a number of ways, in addition to funding them. These include: the development of quality standards, as occurs in the United Kingdom, where all local adult guidance partnerships must adhere to national standards in order to get government funds; the development of a national career information web site including regular references to local services; and helping to co-ordinate web site, help line and face-to-face services.

# CHAPTER 5. WIDENING ACCESS THROUGH INNOVATIVE AND DIVERSE DELIVERY

This chapter highlights a number of ways in which access to career guidance can be widened and in which the needs of more diverse target-groups can be met, on a cost-effective basis. These involve reorganising the work, the adoption of new tools and techniques, and investment in new technologies.

The chapter's key policy conclusions are that:

◆ The labour-intensive nature of face-to-face interviews implies that policy-makers need to seek more innovative and cost-effective ways to provide career guidance if they are to widen access without a large increase in public expenditure.

◆ A number of more cost-effective approaches are available. These include self-help techniques, the creation of open-access resource centres, the use of community members, and wider use of support staff. More flexible approaches to work organisation, including extended hours and outreach methods, can also be used to extend access to career guidance.

◆ ICT has significant potential – still unrealised in many OECD countries – to extend access to career guidance. Present limitations include lack of access to ICT, bandwidth limitations, and lack of staff skills and training.

◆ Call centre technology and help lines also have significant potential to widen access to career guidance, but are under-utilised in most OECD countries.

◆ All of these more innovative and cost-effective ways to deliver career guidance have implications for the training and skills of career guidance practitioners. These need to be addressed by policy-makers if the potential of new approaches is to be more fully realised. They also imply a need for better use of screening processes that allow client needs to be better matched to the services available.

## 5.1. Diversifying service delivery

*Traditional one-to-one interviews are labour-intensive.*

Traditionally, career guidance has been carried out largely through one-to-one interviews. It has been a personal service analogous to hairdressing in its cost structure: productivity gains have been hard to realise. However a need for wider access to career guidance – both throughout the lifespan and by more diverse client groups – focuses attention on how productivity gains can be used to widen access.

*Other strategies, however, are less labour-intensive, but are rarely introduced systematically.*

This review has highlighted the availability of a wide range of strategies and approaches that are less labour-intensive than one-to-one interviews, and that can be used to replace or supplement such interviews. All of them can potentially increase the time that clients are actively involved in career guidance activities in relation to professional staff resources. In many cases, techniques that might widen access, diversify service delivery and allow resources to be better targeted have been adopted in an occasional or one-off manner, often at local level, without being translated into national practice. Policy-makers have rarely taken a systematic approach to the integration of several of these techniques to build more comprehensive and cost-effective career guidance strategies.

*Several techniques are available to diversify delivery methods.*

There are a number of ways in which service delivery can be diversified to use staff time more productively:

- *Embedding career education in the curriculum*. This now occurs in schools in a wide range of OECD countries, and also in tertiary education. Some of the issues involved in a curriculum-based approach are discussed in Chapter 3.

- *Group guidance activities* are commonly used in some career guidance services: for example in Germany's Federal Employment Service; or in the Career Counselling Programme recently established in Australia. For some purposes these may be just as helpful as one-to-one interventions.

- *Self-help techniques* most commonly assess vocational interests, but also competencies, and relate these to possible occupational and educational choices. Originally most self-help tools were developed in paper and pencil format – for example the Holland Self Directed Search (Holland, 1997) – but increasingly self-help tools are being included as part of web-based services. They are able to be scored and interpreted by clients themselves, without, in most cases, intervention by a career guidance practitioner.

- *Reorganising the physical layout of careers centres* as open-access resource centres which clients can use on a self-service basis, with minimal help. This commonly involves services being made available at several levels, from self-help to lengthier interviews. Self-help is normally the initial contact point, supported by appropriately trained receptionists and by clear signs to indicate what resources are available. It is commonly used in many higher education career services in the United Kingdom, and also increasingly in many of the Connexions services for young people in England. It is also common in some countries' public employment services, for example in Austria.

- *Encouraging community members to deliver parts of programmes*: for example, alumni, parents, employers and trade-union representatives can all be involved in giving talks, in mentoring programmes, and in providing work-experience opportunities. Chapter 3 has described some programmes that systematically involve community members in schools.

- *Making use of support staff* to work alongside more highly qualified staff in delivering services, for example, providing help with information searches, and in managing relationships with community members. Generally such support staff have both less, and different, training to fully qualified practitioners. The use of support staff, and more differentiated staffing and qualifications structures, is common in open-access resource centres. This is the case in university careers services in Australia, where there is a mix of career counsellors, information officers and employment officers. A mix is also found in the large (100 or more staff) career guidance organisations in the United Kingdom such as Connexions Services and Careers Wales companies, and in Ireland where adult career guidance services employ information officers alongside guidance counsellors.

## 5.2.    Extending access

*Various strategies are available for extending access.*

Many strategies exist to extend access to services to clients who might not otherwise be able to use them:

- In Germany, the opening hours of some public employment offices are being extended on one or two days a week in order to make them accessible to employed people.

- Outreach approaches, in which services are taken to where clients are, or are located in accessible community settings, are commonly used in a number of countries to widen access to career guidance. For example the strategies for working with out-of-school youth in a number of Scandinavian countries, Ireland and Luxembourg commonly make use of outreach approaches. The Austrian adult guidance pilot programme described in Chapter 4 uses a peripatetic approach to bring services to communities where clients are located, rather than requiring clients to come to a common service centre. A similar peripatetic approach to widening access is used by many of the adult guidance partnerships that operate in England and in Wales.

- One of the rationales for the contracting-out of services to community-based organisations is, as noted in Chapter 4, that they are often perceived by members of their target-groups to be more accessible and more attuned to their needs.

## 5.3. Harnessing technology

*ICT has a potentially important role, and can be used in a wide variety of ways.*

A further strategy both for diversifying service delivery and for extending access is to harness the power of information and communication technologies (ICT). In all countries, ICT is now used extensively in guidance services: frequently as a way of providing career information, but often also to offer other forms of support for career decision-making. ICT can be used in career guidance to achieve a number of purposes:[1]

- *Self-awareness.* These include ICT resources that help users to assess themselves and to develop a profile that can be related to learning and work opportunities. They range from simple self-assessment questionnaires to more sophisticated psychometric tests.

- *Opportunity awareness.* These include databases of learning and work opportunities, with a menu of search criteria which enable users to find the information that they need. The databases may cover: education and training institutions or courses; the content of occupations; employers, or job vacancies; voluntary-work opportunities; information on sources of childcare or income support; and information on how to become self-employed. Some include information on labour-market supply and demand. There are also some examples which let users simulate what it is like to work in particular occupational areas.

- *Decision learning.* These include systems which let users match their personal profiles to learning or work opportunities. The outcome is a list of the opportunities which match the profile most closely. They also include decision-making resources that help users explore options systematically, balancing how attractive options are against the probability of achieving them.

- *Transition learning.* These help users to implement decisions. They may include support in developing action plans, preparing curricula vitae, completing application forms, and preparing for job interviews. They may also include help in obtaining funding for courses of study or for becoming self-employed.

*The Internet has greatly extended access to career guidance resources...*

These different applications can be available on CD-ROM, but are increasingly available on the Internet. When they are on the Internet they can be accessed from a wide variety of locations, including the home. Many computer-aided guidance systems and web sites cover only one or two of the applications described above. Some cover several. This can

---

1.  The following classification, developed originally by Law and Watts (1977), was adapted by Offer (1997) to classify existing European ICT-based resources in the field of career guidance.

extend their value to users considerably, as they can cover more aspects of the career decision-making process.

***...and has massively increased the extent of such resources.***

The Internet has produced a massive increase in the extent and range of such resources. The ease of interconnecting them means that they no longer need to be viewed as separate entities In addition, many guidance services have begun to develop their own web sites, rather than buying ICT-based resources from external suppliers. This lets them deliver some of their services on-line, and customise links so that they meet the distinctive needs of their clients. It allows them to mix their on-line and off-line services in innovative ways (Offer *et al.*, 2001).

***There are still important limitations to the use of ICT, though many are transitional in nature.***

There are still important limitations to the use of ICT in career guidance. These include:

- *Lack of access*, particularly by those who are poor or elderly, and by people in remote areas without telephones.

- *Bandwidth limitations*, and the cost of Internet access, which restrict the range of resources that can be accessed. In Ireland, for example, the cost of Internet access has restricted access to web-based resources, and forced many schools to rely instead upon CD-ROM based guidance materials. These are more costly and slower to update than web-based resources.

- *Lack of skills and training* in the use of ICT on the part of guidance professionals. In many countries, ICT does not appear to attract much attention in career guidance training programmes (McCarthy, 2001).

These limitations restrict the extent to which ICT is used in career guidance in many countries. As an example, in Australia, a government decision to reduce the number of printed copies of its Job Guide because it is available on-line was widely criticised by schools because many students do not have easy access to the Internet at school or at home. The decision was subsequently reversed. In France a survey in 2000 found that many more young people still consulted paper documents than the Internet or CD-ROMs (Tricot, 2002). Many of these limitations are transitional problems, and it seems likely that ICT will continue to grow as a form of service delivery.

***Increasing use is also being made of help lines, though this is under-exploited in many countries.***

Imaginative use can also be made of call centre technology to widen access to career guidance. An important example is outlined in Box 5.1 Other examples include:

- In Australia, the 12 Career Information Centres responded to nearly 40 000 enquiries by telephone in the first six months of 2001. There are also other help line services in the guidance field in Australia. In Victoria, for example, Youth Employment Link has a small call centre with four staff servicing young people aged 15-24. Victoria's TAFE Course Line, which provides information on vocational education and training and has four staff, took over 47 000 calls in 2001. In Western Australia, a Training Information Centre with nine staff takes around 45 000 calls per year. The Tertiary Advice and Counselling Service in Queensland offers telephone advice and counselling on a fee-for-service basis.

- In Canada there is a career information hotline in Alberta.

- Plans to develop call centres for career information or guidance are also under consideration in other countries including Germany, the Netherlands and Norway.

- Some of these services also offer contact by e-mail, fax and post.

Help lines are of particular value in helping to increase access in rural and remote communities, and in increasing access for those who cannot easily visit traditional career guidance centres such as single parents, the disabled, and prisoners. In general help lines are an under-exploited career guidance resource in most countries.

*Help lines, web sites, e-mail and face-to-face career guidance need to be integrated.*

Help lines, web sites and e-mail, linked with face-to-face facilities, open up new opportunities for the delivery of career guidance. People can get help in a convenient form, with which they feel most comfortable. Some feel comfortable visiting a careers centre; some do not. Some are more comfortable on the telephone, or on e-mail; some are not. Public policy should promote opportunities for wider choice in the ways that services can be used.

*ICT is normally used in a stand-alone way.*

It is now possible to use ICT-based services as part of a client-practitioner relationship. However the trend with publicly funded services is towards technology being used in stand-alone ways. These allow standardised services to be used repeatedly by different users without additional staff costs. This adds substantially to the policy options for extending access to services without commensurate increases in costs.

*ICT has implications for career guidance staffing structures and training.*

Where ICT is used in a stand-alone way, career guidance practitioners need to do three things: assess people's needs and indicate the resources and services which might best meet them; be available for brief interventions to help them review what they have learned from these resources and services; and be available for longer interviews for those who need them. The first two of these roles might be performed in part by support staff, with support from fully trained staff. .

The use of ICT requires career guidance practitioners to know how to manage a wider range of career guidance resources. They need to know how to identify which resources are appropriate for different clients, and they need to know how to use these resources appropriately. This includes knowing how to use screening processes. Thus wider use of ICT has the potential to expand opportunities for more differentiated staffing structures to be introduced, and has implications for the types of skills needed by career guidance practitioners.

---

**Box 5.1. The learndirect service in the United Kingdom**

learndirect is a highly innovative approach to meeting the career guidance needs of adults. Its methods of operation are strikingly different from traditional methods based upon 30-minute personal interviews that require clients to make appointments and visit specialised career guidance centres. Launched in 1998, its core is built around call centre technology. There are two call centres in England (in Manchester and Leicester), one for Northern Ireland, and smaller centres in Scotland and Wales. Its underlying goal is to offer free and impartial advice that can assist adults to access further education and training opportunities. To support advice and information on learning opportunities, learndirect provides information on funding for learning and on childcare. learndirect is open to all adults, but like a number of other recent initiatives in the United Kingdom, it focuses particularly upon adults with low levels of qualifications. Call centre help lines are open between 8.00 and 22.00, 365 days a year. This makes the service accessible well outside of standard business hours, and makes it easily accessible by groups such as prisoners, those of no fixed abode, foreign students, the isolated, and asylum seekers. Over five million people have called learndirect since it was opened.

Staff have to be prepared to do shift work. In addition, around a quarter of all staff work part-time. Call centres are staffed by Information Advisers who act as the first point of contact and handle basic information inquiries. The next level of staff, known as Learning Advisers, handles the inquiries of those who need more than basic information. A third tier of staff, known as Lifelong Learning Advisers, handles more complex inquiries and requests for help. As a rough indication, calls handled by Information Advisers last an average of 3.5 minutes, calls handled by Learning Advisers an average of 8.5 minutes, and calls handled by Lifelong Learning Advisers an average of 16 minutes. Demand for the services of Lifelong Learning Advisers is substantially above their capacity to handle them. Special training programmes and qualifications have been devised or adapted for learndirect staff, as it has been found that standard qualifications do not easily fit its needs. Initially some career guidance practitioners had expressed reservations about whether the type of work being conducted within learndirect could be described as career guidance. However initial suspicions appear to have considerably reduced.

All staff have access to an online database of information on some 600 000 education and training courses, at all levels, as well as a wide variety of other printed information. The online database can be accessed directly at *www.learndirect.co.uk/*, and is updated monthly. An online diagnostic package can be used to assess interests and preferences as part of the web site. There have been over 10 million hits on the site since it opened in 2000.

In order to attract callers, learndirect conducts regular and systematic marketing campaigns. These make heavy use of radio and television, and can be targeted at particular occupations or themes. Experienced marketing staff are employed to buy advertising time and space for this purpose.

learndirect is discussed in Watts and Dent (2002).

---

## 5.4. Screening processes

*Screening processes are needed to identify client needs and how they can be met.*

The wider use of self-help tools, the introduction of open-access resource centres, and some of the ways in which ICT can be used in career guidance all increase the need for screening processes or tools. These allow clients to be sorted into priority groups according to their needs, and more costly intensive services to be provided for those who need them. Screening tools have been developed within public employment services, although in practice administratively simpler criteria such as unemployment duration are often used to allocate services.

Some employment services have adopted a three-level service model to ensure that intensive assistance is provided to the most needy and to high priority groups:

- In Germany, unemployed adults are required to have an interview with a placement officer to estimate their chances of reintegration into the labour market, and to assess what help they need. In some cases they are then expected to find a job on their own by using the service's do-it-yourself information facilities; others are provided with brief help or are given help in groups; others are referred to a counsellor for more intensive help.

- In the Netherlands, the operating principle in the new Centres for Work and Income is to make sure that people help themselves as much as possible. A three-level model is being developed: for those who can help themselves; for those who need some help; and for those who need a lot of help.

- In the United States, the One-Stop Centres are designed so that all users have access to information; those unable to find jobs then get limited guidance in the use of this information; and those still unable to find jobs get more intensive services including job-search assistance (Grubb, 2002b).

*Both theoretical rationales and practical tools exist to support screening processes.*

There are good grounds for arguing for the use of more differentiated career guidance methods to match different individual needs (Holland, 1997). Screening tools can be a way to do this, as well as to ensure that the most effective use is made of staff time. Although they are not yet common, a rationale for the use of such tools within such three-level models has been developed by Sampson and his colleagues (Sampson, Palmer and Watts, 1999; Sampson *et al.*, 1999) in terms of readiness for decision-making. Thus:

- Those who are initially judged to have a *high* level of readiness for career decision-making can be referred to *self-help* services: career resource rooms and web sites designed to help them to select, find, sequence and use resources with little or no help.

- Those judged to have a *moderate* level of readiness can be referred to brief *staff-assisted* services: some help with the use of resources, supplemented by group sessions.

- Those with a *low* level of readiness can be referred to *individual case-managed* services: individual counselling and longer-term group counselling.

A range of instruments to measure readiness for career decision-making exist. These include measures of career certainty or indecision, of vocational identity, and of dysfunctional career thoughts. Estimates of the proportion of people who need individual, case-managed services tend to fall between 10% and 50%, depending on the population, with the remainder being divided between those requiring self-help and brief staff-assisted services (Sampson *et al.*, 1999). Earlier estimates using a paper-and-pencil-based tool (Holland, 1997) led to a similar conclusion: perhaps only 30% of people need individual case-managed career guidance. Such findings have significant implications for policy-makers seeking to judge the level of resources that need to be invested in lifelong career guidance systems. Chapter 10 returns to this point.

# CHAPTER 6. PROVIDING CAREER INFORMATION MORE EFFECTIVELY

This chapter discusses why the quality and availability of career information matter as policy issues. It outlines the principal sources of career information and their strengths and limitations, and discusses what needs to be done to ensure that it is used, once produced.

The chapter's key policy conclusions are that:

♦ Good career information is essential for good quality career guidance.

♦ In many OECD countries career information is not well co-ordinated between different ministries and agencies or between different levels of government. This limits its transparency and comprehensiveness. In particular, educational, occupational and labour market supply and demand information are too often separated, and too infrequently linked to self-assessment tools.

♦ Too often career information is provider-driven rather than user-driven. It needs to be more thoroughly based upon client needs and upon what is known about the career decision-making process. In addition, it is often stronger in providing educational information than in providing occupational and labour market information, and too infrequently reports the labour market destinations of graduates from educational institutions.

♦ ICT has the potential to address many of these problems. However a simple replication, on-line or in CD-ROM format, of existing print-based sources is a major waste of this potential.

♦ In addition to ensuring that career information is comprehensive, impartial and integrated, governments have a responsibility to set standards for the wider market for career information, including that which is produced by the private sector. They also need to consider how career information is used, once produced.

## 6.1.    Why career information matters

*Good-quality career information is essential for good-quality career guidance.*

The key theories of vocational choice and development that underpin career guidance have long ascribed a central role to information. Information – about the self, about education and training opportunities, about occupations and their characteristics, about labour market supply and demand – is central to notions such as the self concept and career decidedness. The skills that people have in gathering, evaluating and applying such information in order to manage their careers are keys to concepts such as vocational maturity, which in turn underpin the rationale for different types of career guidance interventions (see Killeen, 1996b). Labour economists view information that is accurate and equally available – about workers' attributes, about the availability and characteristics of jobs – as a key to labour market efficiency: as indeed it is to the efficiency of all types of markets (Grubb, 2002a). Where information is imperfect or asymmetric the efficiency of job searches and of matches between labour supply and labour demand is reduced (Autor, 2001).

People obtain the educational, occupational and labour market information that they need from a wide variety of sources. Some of these are informal: family and friends for example. Such sources are likely to be well trusted and rich in detail, but may also be partial and unreliable. They may fail to open up new possibilities for exploration, confining people to the known and familiar. For comprehensive, impartial and reliable information, and to widen the chances that information will open up new options, people have to look to more formal sources. Career information, then, is a central part of career guidance. The quality of career information, its effective organisation and distribution and its accessibility must be seen as important issues for public policy.

## 6.2.    Sources of career information

*Since career information is a public good, governments need to make sure that it is available.*

Career information is widely recognised as a public good which should be freely available to all, for reasons of both efficiency and equity. This is why governments play an important role in providing formal career information. In some countries, the role that should be played by governments has been made explicit. In Canada, for example, career and labour market information is officially viewed as being "important because it enables Canadians, including employers, workers, job seekers and educational institutions, to make a range of informed labour market decisions".

Career information is produced in a very wide variety of formats: comprehensive occupational guides containing information on the content of many hundreds of occupations and their education and training requirements; individual leaflets or brochures on particular occupations or industries; handbooks and catalogues produced by educational institutions, as well as collective guides to courses and institutions in particular sectors of education or regions; and promotional material produced by individual enterprises or industry associations. Increasingly it is available electronically: on CD-ROMs; in the form of videos and films; and on the Internet.

*Some governments have set up specialist agencies for this purpose.*

In most countries, governments play a significant role in funding the collection, organisation, linking, systematising and distribution of career information. They do this in a variety of ways. In a few cases they have set up separate agencies to do it:

- In France three national agencies play a role in collecting, producing and disseminating career information: the *Office National d'Information sur les Enseignements et les Professions* (ONISEP), which was created in 1970; *le Centre d'Information et de Documentation Jeunesse* (CIDJ), which was created in 1969; and the *Centre pour le Développement de l'Information sur la Formation Permanente* (le centre INFFO), which was created in 1976.

- In Denmark the National Council for Educational and Vocational Guidance (RUE) has had a similar set of responsibilities, although this body is now being replaced.

- In the United States, a National Occupational Information Coordinating Committee was set up in 1976 to build a national network of State Occupational Information Coordinating Committees (SOICCs), and to construct a national framework for state-specific occupational information systems (NOICC, 2000). In 2000, new vocational education legislation transferred NOICC's functions to the United States Department of Education.

- In the Netherlands, linked to the privatisation of guidance agencies, the education and employment ministries in 1992 transferred many of their information and materials-development activities to the National Career Service Centre (LDC). Initially LDC was fully subsidised by the government, but these subsidies have gradually been reduced, being replaced by sales of products (particularly from schools and also from human resource departments within companies) and contracts for particular activities. From the end of 2002 the subsidies have disappeared altogether.

One advantage of such agencies is that they can more easily co-ordinate the collection of information: across portfolios – particularly education and labour; across different sectors of education; and between different levels of government administration such as state and national governments. Such agencies also make it easier to link different types of information, or to compile it in a single source. Without such agencies, governments must address these co-ordination issues in other ways.

*More often, individual ministries produce career information or contract out its production.*

More commonly, the production and distribution of career information is the responsibility of individual ministries, either directly or through contracting out to the private sector. In Australia, much national career information is based on partnerships between government and the private sector. The private-sector Good Guides Group, in particular, has contracts to supply a number of key products, including the *Job Guide* which is disseminated to all schools, and the OZJAC computer-based information system which is also widely used in schools. In Australia the government also funds sector bodies in industries experiencing skill shortages to produce innovative career information. Government financial support to private-sector information products is also provided, for example, in Canada, Germany and Ireland.

*There is a variety of other information providers…*

Other significant information suppliers include educational institutions, industry associations and enterprises. Where individual organisations publish information, whether in print, video, or on-line, it is usually designed to be persuasive, and to serve promotional purposes. Where the information is published under a collective umbrella, it may be more objective. In several countries, for example the United Kingdom, comprehensive objective listings of higher education courses are provided by universities' representative bodies.

Other organisations may publish information from a consumer perspective:

- In the United Kingdom, some students' unions have published alternative prospectuses, for potential students to use alongside official prospectuses.

- In several countries, newspapers publish ratings of higher education institutions from a consumer perspective.

- In the Netherlands, students entering higher education have access to systematic information on current students' ratings, by institution and subject, of their programme, their teachers, and the facilities provided for them. The publication of this information is supported by government funding.

*…including the private sector.*

In many countries, there is also a private sector in career information, including guides, handbooks, books on occupations, web sites and the like. Some are financed by sales to users; some by advertisements (whether overt or disguised in an editorially controlled form); some by a mix of both. Where products are funded in whole or in part by providers who pay for editorial entries, this may restrict the comprehensiveness and impartiality of the information, and this may not be evident to users. It is also common in some countries for major metropolitan newspapers to produce regular careers supplements, often containing personalised depictions of occupations or job sectors of a type that is often not available in more formal government guides, and funded through advertisements. An example of a career information product produced for the private market in Ireland is described in Box 6.1.

---

Box 6.1. **A private sector career information product in Ireland**

*Careers World* is a widely used career information product that was developed by the private sector with financial support from the Department of Education and Science. Available on the Internet at *www.careersworld.com/* and distributed free to schools and other educational institutions in CD-ROM format, *Careers World* draws its information from enterprises, most of which are large and in the private sector, and enables them to provide information on the employment and careers that they offer. It is funded by employer subscriptions, and has been seen as a way for firms to help recruit staff in a tight labour market. Whether it will continue to enjoy the same level of employer support in a labour market less marked by skill shortages is a key question for its future.

Its coverage of small firms, which form the majority of the Irish enterprises, is limited, as is its coverage of some occupational areas. It includes a preference assessment exercise, and has a polished and professional feel to it, with ample graphics and sound. It also provides links to tertiary and further education course information related to the occupational areas that it includes. The principal feature that it contains which is not found in the other main products available in Ireland is its "real life" component: exemplars of individuals who are working in the contributing enterprises.

---

The private sector is also active in producing much career information on the Internet. An example is JobStar Central (*jobstar.org/jobstar.cfm*), originally funded through a United States federal government grant, supported through the Wall Street Journal's careers site, and providing users with access to a recruitment database as well as to occupational and education and training information. In the United States many of the educational portals which provide information on college entry mirror the market that has long existed for such private guides in print form. An example is *www.petersons.com/*.

## 6.3. Gaps and weaknesses in career information

*Fragmented career information is common where separate ministries and government agencies are not well co-ordinated.*

If good co-ordination does not exist, fragmented responsibility for career information between different ministries or agencies can result in lack of transparency and fragmentation of the information itself. For example in Spain it is common for products that give information on courses of education and training to be published separately by the individual autonomous communities, which have legal responsibility for the provision of education. It is also common, within individual autonomous communities, for separate guides to be produced for the different sectors of education and training. Whilst the creation of a single national system of vocational education qualifications, in place of the previous three, has helped to reduce this fragmentation, it is still common for separate guides to be produced for vocational education and tertiary education. In Ireland, separate information products have been produced for tertiary and post-secondary courses of education, for vocational training, and for adult education. In Austria a growing interest in producing on-line databases of adult education courses initially resulted in many regions producing their own, unconnected databases. Steps have been taken to connect these separate databases. In Norway, there are a number of overlapping databases on adult education, which together provide only partial coverage of what is available.

It is also common for products that contain information on education and training courses to be separated from sources of information on the content of the jobs that these qualifications lead to. In Finland, for example, at the time of the OECD review, the main national product containing information on the training needed in order to become a carpenter was separate from the product containing information on the content of the occupation of carpenter. Each, in turn, was separate from the major sources of information on labour market supply and demand for carpenters. Similar fragmentation between education and training information, occupational information and labour market information was observed in a number of other countries. In Germany, the Federal Employment Service currently has separate databases on occupations (BerufeNET), on training opportunities (KURS), on apprenticeship and training vacancies (ASIS), and on job vacancies (SIS); these are distinct from a career selection programme (MACH'S RICHTIG) and other self-exploration programmes. Work has started to transfer these to the Internet in a more integrated form.

Fragmented career information such as the above examples can make it difficult for people to get a comprehensive overview of what is available. This has implications both for geographical mobility and for social mobility. Lack of transparency, and difficulty in obtaining integrated information, suit existing separate administrative boundaries. However they fail to deliver the comprehensive information that people need to make career decisions (Tricot, 2002).

*Too much information is provider- rather than customer-driven.*

The production of career information to reflect existing bureaucratic boundaries rather than consumer need reflects a wider issue: in general, much of the available career information is provider-driven rather than customer-driven. There is a need for more customer-oriented portals and search engines, working from questions which individuals want to ask, rather than from the information which providers want them to have. There is also a need for the design of career information products to be more thoroughly grounded in what is known from research about the career development and decision-making processes. Box 6.3 below provides an example of a career information product that has taken this into account.

*The quality of labour market information is strong in some countries…*

Information on labour market supply and demand, including local and regional information as well as national information, is an essential element of career information. The quality of labour market information varies across countries. It is particularly strong in Canada (Box 6.2). Other examples exist of good practice:

- In Korea, materials produced by the Work Information Centre of the Korea Human Resource Development Service include: occupational classifications and statistics; the KNOW (Korea Network for Occupations and Workers) system of occupational profiles covering worker interests, skills, aptitudes and other requirements, plus salaries and prospects (to be completed in 2003, based on the O*NET system in the United States); and occupational outlook data (Korean Job Future, revised every two years) comprising five-year forecasts based on extensive employment surveys. The latter publication is sent to schools and universities, along with other creative resources including a job game developed for use in elementary schools (further versions for junior high and senior high schools are being developed).

- In the Netherlands, a database of projected labour-market demand in some 2 500 occupations has been developed, linked to related education and training routes.

*...but relatively weak in others.*

In countries like Denmark, Luxembourg and Norway, however, little information seems currently to be provided to schools and other guidance services on supply and demand in different occupational areas, or on salaries and wages.

---

**Box 6.2. Labour market information in Canada**

The collection and analysis of labour market information is a major activity in the public employment services in Canada. Human Resources Development Canada (HRDC) has a legal responsibility for information on jobs, occupations, career paths and learning opportunities, as well as labour market trends.

In addition to using its own internal resources to develop and disseminate this information, HRDC supports a number of partnerships with the provinces to co-ordinate their efforts in this area. These include the Canada Career Consortium (CCC), the Canadian Career Information Partnership (CCIP) and Canada WorkInfoNet (CANWIN). These arrangements co-ordinate data-collection systems which are rightly claimed to be among the best in the world. CANWIN is responsible for a national portal designed to connect all citizens to the career information they need; it is based on a lead partner in each province, working within a set of common guidelines (in these respects it bears some resemblances to the ESTIA network in the European Union).

One of the key products from HRDC's labour market information work is *Job Futures*, which is extensively used by career guidance practitioners and their clients. It includes supply and demand projections by occupation and by field of study, and is accompanied by a guide to help practitioners answer common labour market information questions. In future these products will be available in web-based form only, making it easier to update them. Provinces also create their own parallel products.

---

*There are arguments for attempting to base labour market information more on skills and competencies, and to pay more attention to career paths.*

There is concern in several countries that existing labour market information does not capture changes within occupations and is slow in capturing and describing new occupations. If labour market information could be based more flexibly on skills and competencies, rather than upon occupations alone, this might make it easier to update. It might also help people to consider moves across occupational boundaries, so enabling them to adapt more easily to declining demand in existing occupations or the opening up of new occupations. More information also needs to be provided on career paths within and across occupations.

*More attention is also needed to local differences.*

Another common criticism of labour market information is that it tends to be national or at best regional in nature, and to pay insufficient attention to differences between local labour markets. Rural and remote areas may be particularly poorly served in these respects.

*Another significant gap is information on course destinations.*

A significant information gap in most countries is information on the destinations of students from different tertiary education courses. Several countries (including Australia, Canada, Korea, Norway and the United Kingdom) conduct regular surveys of such destinations, but in general the results are not made available in a user-friendly form on a course-by-course basis. Yet post-course destinations, preferably a couple of years after graduation as well as in the immediate post-graduation period, represent important information for students considering entry to such courses, enabling them to evaluate the extent and nature of the employment prospects to which the courses lead. Particularly in countries where students and their families are increasingly expected to cover or contribute to their tuition and living costs, there is likely to be growing demand for such information.

This gap is an illustration of two more general points: that educational information is often better-developed than occupational information; and that these two forms of information are often only weakly linked.

---

Box 6.3. **The National Career Information System in Australia**

A major recent initiative in Australia has been the establishment of a National Career Information System (NCIS), which is designed to provide a comprehensive web-based career exploration and information service for all Australians (*www.myfuture.edu.au/*). It represents a significant co-operative venture between the federal and state governments (previously the states adopted very different approaches to the delivery of career information), plus a variety of other partners. The development costs were met by the federal government; recurrent costs will be shared between the federal government and the states.

The system contains information on education and training opportunities and on occupations, including regional information on labour-market demand and on wages and salaries (drawn from census data). It also includes opportunities for users to assess their interests and capabilities and match these to potential occupations.

In addition, there are sections designed to build the helping capacity of parents and other career "influencers". Attention is given to adult career development themes such as life balance and mid-life career change alongside the more familiar focus on employment search. A rationale paper (McMahon and Tatham, 2002) published to accompany the launch of the system locates it in relation to the wider processes of career guidance and career development.

---

*ICT offers new possibilities for career information provision...*

Much career information is now ICT-based, either on CD-ROM or, increasingly, on the Internet. This has many advantages:

- It is easy to link different types of information: information on education and training, on the labour market, on the content of jobs. Thus ICT offers an opportunity to address the common problem of poorly integrated career information discussed above. An example of an integrated system is described in Box 6.3.

- The information can be updated quickly and at minimal cost, especially when web-based.

- The information can be readily linked to personal assessment tools.

- The information can be designed so that it is easier for individuals to search and navigate through it than in the case of print-based career information.

Governments seem increasingly to be attracted to ICT applications. This is partly because it is more cost-effective. It is also sometimes linked to their strategies for promoting e-learning and the ICT capability of their citizens.

*...but often this potential is not fully harnessed.*

At present, however, many ICT-based career information systems are replicas of print-based systems, and so do not use the new opportunities which ICT offers. Too often, as well, insufficient attention is given in the design of systems to considering how and for what purposes they are to be used. In particular, techniques to enable users to link their personal characteristics to career information are commonly crude or not sufficiently developed.

*Governments have an interest in the quality of all career information, whatever its source.*

Many of the gaps and weaknesses in career information outlined above could be addressed by wider use of information quality standards. In view of governments' interest in the quality of career information as a public good, and the diversity of sources of such information, there is a case for governments to extend their role beyond being one of the providers, and also to set standards for all types of career information. These could cover such criteria as: its accuracy; its comprehensiveness; its relevance to the target-group (including its usability and its tested reading levels); its objectivity and freedom from bias; and the extent to which it is up-to-date (Tricot, 2002).

*Some countries have developed standards for career information.*

A number of countries have developed standards of this kind, either as a government initiative or as an initiative of career guidance representative organisations. In the United States, standards have been developed by the National Career Development Association for career information literature, for video career media, for software, and for web sites. The first of these sets the model for the others to some extent. It contains, among its general guidelines, a list of items to help editors of career information: dating and revisions, credits, accuracy of information, format, vocabulary, use of information, bias and stereotyping, and graphics, followed by comprehensive content guidelines (see Plant, 2001). Guidelines for career information have also been developed in Denmark and the Netherlands and are currently being developed in Canada. At present, all such guidelines operate on a voluntary basis.

## 6.4.    Converting information into action

*Information is necessary for good career decision-making, but it is not sufficient. Reasons include...*

Public investment in information is of little value if its potential users are not able to access the information they require, to understand it and relate it to their personal needs, and to act upon it. Many people cannot do so. There is clearly a need for more research in this area, including research on how people find and use information. Meanwhile there are good grounds for believing that information, while necessary, is not sufficient, in at least three respects.

*...equity of access...*

The first is equity of access. Most information requires good reading skills, and is not accessible to those who cannot read well. In addition, information has tended to be more accessible to people in urban than in rural areas. As more information is delivered in electronic form, this marginalises those who do not have access to ICT or do not have the skills or confidence to use it effectively.

*...difficulties in finding the information one needs...*

The second is difficulties in finding the right information. Most people are now faced with too much information. They often access and sift information in very ad hoc rather than systematic ways. Often people look for information only at the last minute, taking the quickest and easiest source they can find. This means that they may be influenced by information that they find by chance rather than by a systematic search of a reasonably comprehensive range of information.

*...and the need expressed by many for personal support...*

The third is the need to "talk it through" with someone. Many people feel a need to discuss information with someone before they can act upon it. This may be a friend or relation. It may be someone who is knowledgeable, such as a person who actually works in an occupation. At times it will be a career guidance practitioner who can help them to relate information to their needs and to act upon it.

*...which is linked to the complex and personal nature of career decision-making, compared with consumer choices.*

This is linked to a more fundamental point. As Grubb (2002a) points out:

> "In many respects the choices about schooling, work, and careers are not choices in the same sense that we think of the choices among shirts or fruit or financial services; they are much more difficult issues of identity, involving deeper issues of what a person is, what their values are, how they position themselves with respect to others and to social groups, what they think of as a worthy life – the many different elements defining who they are."

*Strategies for providing information need to be linked to strategies for using it.*

Policies for developing career information need to pay attention both to its production and distribution, and to how it can be made relevant and meaningful, and used. Austria provides two examples of systematic attempts to communicate career information so that it is placed in context and made more meaningful to users. The first, outlined in Chapter 3, is an extensive programme organised by the Austrian National Union of Students in which tertiary students visit final year (grade 12) school classes to provide information on university study and assist the transition to university life. This programme complements printed material on entry requirements and course content published by the Ministry for Education, Science and Culture. The second is a programme that operates in the career information centre (BIZ) of the Economic Chamber of Vienna. Here, an extensive collection of printed and electronic information is available on a wide range of occupations. To complement this, and to help make it more meaningful to young people, the centre maintains a network of employers to whom young people can be referred for personal discussion and to see what is actually done in jobs.

# CHAPTER 7. STAFFING CAREER GUIDANCE

This chapter outlines some of the difficulties involved in trying to assess the size of the career guidance workforce. The non-specialised basis upon which career guidance is often delivered, the weak training and qualification arrangements that exist in most countries, and the fragmented nature of practitioner representative organisations indicate that career guidance is almost everywhere weakly professionalised. In many countries insufficient training, inappropriate training, or both, constitute significant barriers to the capacity of career guidance services to contribute to the implementation of lifelong learning and active labour market policies. The chapter argues for a stronger role for governments in setting training standards and content.

The chapter's key policy conclusions are that:

♦   Using the standard criteria for a profession, career guidance is weakly professionalised in most countries. In the largest settings in which it is typically provided (schools and public employment services) it is commonly provided by people who are also expected to do other things (teach, place people in jobs, help people with personal and study problems) and who normally do not have specialised tertiary-level qualifications and training for their career guidance work.

♦   Career guidance practitioners in many countries receive either insufficient or inappropriate training. Available training programmes generally have major gaps in a number of areas that are important for the capacity of career guidance to meet the types of policy challenges outlined at the beginning of this report. In particular they are weak in: developing skills in ICT use in career guidance; training for support workers; providing an understanding of labour market changes; developing skills for curriculum-based delivery; teaching practitioners how to develop clients' career self-management skills; and teaching practitioners how to organise and manage career guidance resources, as opposed to direct personal service delivery.

♦   Governments need to play a more direct role in reshaping the nature of the career guidance workforce and its qualification and training arrangements. A priority in most countries should be to create separate, and appropriate, occupational and organisational structures through which career guidance can be delivered, including more differentiated occupational structures. This needs to be combined with significant improvements to the level of training required of career guidance practitioners, and with more deliberate interventions to shape the content and nature of career guidance training.

♦   Comprehensive competency frameworks, covering both support staff and fully qualified staff, need to be developed as a basis for these types of reforms.

## 7.1.    How large is the career guidance workforce?

*Information on career guidance practitioners is difficult to obtain.*

Information on the size and nature of the career guidance workforce is difficult to obtain in all countries. Where data is available its reliability and interpretation are often uncertain, and it is rarely comparable across countries. These problems arise for a number of reasons. Unlike many other services, career guidance is not always provided on a full-time specialist basis by people who have specialised and officially recognised qualifications. Clear entry and qualification routes into clearly defined occupational roles are often absent. The career guidance workforce includes many whose primary occupational identity is not as a career guidance specialist but as a teacher, psychologist, counsellor, human resource specialist, employment officer or labour-market analyst, for example. Often they provide career guidance for only part of their working time. In schools, career guidance is commonly regarded as a specialist sub-role for selected teachers, often with limited time to carry it out, and with limited training, possibly on a voluntary basis.

As a result of how career guidance is provided, headcounts may include those who provide career guidance as only part of their duties, those who provide it as their principal duty, or both. In assessing the size of national career guidance workforces, it is difficult, as an example, to directly compare an Austrian teacher who has undertaken a brief in-service training course and who is given one to two hours release each week to provide both educational and career guidance, with an employee of Careers Wales in the United Kingdom who provides career guidance on a full-time basis, and has a specialised postgraduate career guidance qualification. An additional problem in obtaining data is that the career guidance workforce is very diverse, and spread across many different sectors. Thus information may be readily available for some sectors, but not for others. A further problem in attempting to define the size of the career guidance workforce is that in many countries policy-makers have, to date, not seen the need to do so.

*Estimates of the size of the career guidance workforce differ widely, but may have an upper bound of around 0.8% of the labour force.*

Countries taking part in the OECD review were asked to provide the best available data on the total number of people employed to provide career guidance. Only two – Canada and Denmark – were able to provide comprehensive data. The Canadian data comes from a 1994 national survey of "career and employment counsellors", the only comprehensive national source of data available in that country. It shows the estimated total number of career guidance workers to be around 0.68% of the total labour force at the time. That survey was criticised by many in the community sector, who believed that it did not accurately capture the level of their training. It included many in the education sector who provided career guidance for only a relatively small proportion of their time, and many employment counsellors who spent significant time on benefit and employment programme administration. It excluded career guidance practitioners in universities. Denmark estimated that "approximately 22 500 persons are occupied with educational and vocational guidance, typically as a part-time job", and that half of these are located in compulsory education where on average they devote seven hours a week to counselling. The 22 500 represents roughly 0.79% of the total labour force.

In the case of four other countries, data contained within the national questionnaire allowed approximate estimates of workforce size to be calculated. In all cases they were substantially smaller than the Canadian and Danish estimates. The Australian estimate was the lowest of the four, and represented only 0.03% of the labour force. However it was based upon the number of full-time-equivalent positions rather than the total number. Therefore it cannot be compared to the Canadian and Danish figures, even putting aside the different sectors covered (for example it included university career guidance staff, who were excluded from the Canadian survey). Luxembourg provided a total number of career guidance workers that was equal to 0.12% of the labour force. However it should be noted that it is very difficult to estimate the real size of the Luxembourg labour force, as cross-border workers resident in other countries, and resident foreigners mostly working in international organisations, constitute around 62% of total employment.

## 7.2.    Is career guidance a role, an occupation or a profession?

*A profession can be distinguished from an occupation on a number of criteria.*

A profession can be distinguished from an occupation on a number of criteria. These include:

- The existence of clear, formal, specialised and lengthy entry and qualification routes into clearly defined occupational roles, staffed by (generally full-time) specialists.

- Control, or substantial influence, over occupational supply: for example by licensing.

- The existence of standards to control professional behaviour, such as codes of ethics to protect the public interest.

- The use of evidence as basis of practice, combined with clear knowledge of the effects of treatments.

- The existence of a network of supporting professional associations, training institutions and research organisations.

*In most countries career guidance is weakly professionalised.*

On most of these criteria, with only a few exceptions the career guidance workforce is weakly professionalised in most countries. To illustrate this, Annex 3 describes for 14 countries the work roles, training and qualifications of two key sets of career guidance workers: those who provide personal career guidance in and for schools; and those who provide personal career guidance in and for the public employment service.[1] It shows that in most cases, career guidance in and for these two settings is not a specialised function. More commonly, it is provided on a part-time basis by those who are teachers or employment officers: for example in schools in Austria, Denmark and Norway. When provided by full-time guidance specialists, it is frequently combined with other forms of guidance, counselling and personal assistance: the remediation of learning difficulties; the resolution of behavioural and social problems; or job placement. Examples include student counsellors in Finnish schools, some guidance counsellors in Irish secondary schools (others are part-time), counsellors in Spanish schools, and some employment service officers in Ireland's Training and Employment Agency.

There are some exceptions. For example full-time career guidance specialists are employed: in the United Kingdom in Connexions services, Careers Wales and the Careers Service in Northern Ireland; in Germany's Federal Employment Service; in Finland's public employment service; in secondary schools in the Australian state of New South Wales; and in Dutch reintegration companies.

*Career guidance training and qualifications are rarely both specialised and at tertiary level.*

With very few exceptions, the career guidance workforce consists in all countries of people with a tertiary qualification. However that qualification may not have been the basis upon which they entered career guidance, and it may not have been how they acquired the knowledge and skills needed to provide career guidance. The training that is received by those who provide career guidance reinforces the argument that, in most cases, career guidance is a weakly professionalised occupation. Examination of data on the training and qualifications of those who provide career guidance in and for schools and public employment services (Annex 3) suggests that five main training and qualification models exist:

*1. Specialised career guidance qualifications*
Specialised, tertiary-level qualifications in career guidance are required in only a small number of cases. For example: generally in the United Kingdom for those providing personal career guidance to schools; for some of those who work in Germany's Federal Employment Service; for many of those employed to deliver Australia's Career Counselling Programme; and for many of the qualified teachers appointed as careers advisers in schools in New South Wales in Australia (although in-service training can be accepted instead of specialised postgraduate career guidance qualifications).

---

1.    Outside of these two contexts – for example in the community sector or in tertiary education – the nature of training and qualification arrangements, and the ways that these intersect with the organisation of work roles, are even more diverse, and correspondingly harder to summarise systematically. In the case of teachers who deliver career guidance through the curriculum, in the ways outlined in Chapter 3, specific career guidance training arrangements and qualifications requirements (that is, apart from their general training as teachers) are often even weaker than those described here for staff who provide personal career guidance in and for schools.

*Often career guidance forms part of general guidance and counselling training.*

## 2. General counselling and guidance qualifications

In some cases a postgraduate qualification in guidance or counselling is required, but career guidance may form only part of more general training in guidance and counselling. This is the case with the guidance officers in Ireland's schools, student counsellors in Finnish schools, many guidance counsellors in Canadian schools, and many career counsellors' qualifications in Korea.

*Required qualifications can be too general, and insufficient.*

## 3. Basic and general, but insufficient, qualifications

In many cases those who provide personal career guidance, either in schools or in public employment services, are required to have tertiary qualifications in broad fields that are linked to career guidance, but which need not provide any specific training in career guidance itself. The most common case is a requirement for career guidance practitioners to have a qualification in psychology or pedagogy, at either first degree or masters level. In such cases there is normally no requirement for the content of this qualification to provide any exposure either to the specific theories or the specific methods of career guidance. Specific knowledge of the career guidance theories and methods that are needed to underpin its practice in such cases is either (unjustifiably) assumed, or, in rarer instances, provided, often at a fairly superficial level, through in-service training. Qualifications in psychology, or pedagogy, without specific requirements for training in career guidance, are required of those in Austria's School Psychology Service, of school psychologists in the Czech Republic and Luxembourg, school counsellors in Spain, employment service counsellors in the Czech Republic, and vocational guidance psychologists in Finland's employment service. In addition to resulting in insufficient training, possible consequences of such recruitment criteria are that career guidance staff can adopt an inappropriate diagnostic and therapeutic model; or that career guidance can be seen as something for those who have problems, not an entitlement for all who wish it.

*Training may be limited to short tertiary courses…*

## 4. Limited training

In some cases people are appointed to provide career guidance with no specific training in it, and then undertake relatively brief courses run by tertiary education institutions. This is the case for part-time guidance counsellors in Danish schools who undertake relatively brief courses run by tertiary education institutions, and employment officers in Ireland who have the opportunity to undertake a part-time certificate-level course at the University of Maynooth.

*…or may simply be in-service.*

## 5. In-service training

In many cases people are appointed to career guidance roles with no specific training in career guidance and then provided with relatively brief in-service training that leads to no formal qualifications. This is the case with student advisers in Austrian schools, many *schooldekanen* in the Netherlands, guidance counsellors in Norwegian schools, and employment service officers in Austria, Denmark, Korea, Luxembourg, and Norway.

*Many of these training models coexist within the one country.*

It is not unusual for many of these qualification and training models to coexist within the one country. In Australia, for example, the training and qualification standards in different sectors conspicuously lack any coherence or consistency. They range from technical and further education (TAFE) institutes and Queensland schools, where career counselling is offered by registered psychologists who arguably are over- or inappropriately qualified for the task, to other sectors where no qualifications are specified at all. In Korea, career counsellors often seem to have high levels of educational qualifications, but not necessarily to have had substantial training designed to develop their specific competencies in career guidance. Master's degrees in counselling, for example, may include at most one or two courses in career development. Moreover, it seems not uncommon in Korea for roles to be allocated to people with little or no specific training: this is the case, for instance, with some school counsellors and also for the staff of job information centres in higher education.

*In schools, qualification and training levels tend to be higher when the role is given to non-teachers.*

Within schools, qualification and training levels tend to be higher when career guidance roles are allocated to non-teachers. In Australia (Queensland), guidance officers cover both career guidance and personal counselling. They have postgraduate master's-level qualifications in educational psychology, though their training does not necessarily include any significant attention to career guidance. In Canada (Quebec), guidance counsellors in schools must have a master's degree which includes significant attention to career issues, but do not have to have a teaching background. In the Netherlands, a number of schools have now appointed as *schooldekanen* staff who are trained career counsellors but are not teachers – partly perhaps because they tend to be cheaper, but partly also because of their specialised expertise.

*Professionalisation tends to be weaker within higher education.*

Ironically, recruitment, training and qualification standards for career guidance tend to be weak in the sector of education which is responsible for much of the training in the field as a whole: higher education. This tendency has been observed both in other international studies (Watts and van Esbroeck, 1998) and in the OECD review. For example:

- In Denmark, the main form of training for study advisers in higher education used to be short one-week courses. A 1996 review found that only 40% had even attended these courses (Plant, 1998). The length of the courses has since been increased to four weeks.

- In Germany, the guidance staff in the central student counselling services within higher education come from a variety of academic backgrounds; some have specific qualifications in guidance and counselling, but some do not.

- In Ireland, the qualifications and training of the staff of careers services in tertiary education are determined by the institutions themselves, without central regulation.

- The same is true in Canada, apart from Quebec (where career guidance qualifications are strongly protected). In the other provinces, many institutions have not specified the competencies required of guidance specialists, or the training necessary to acquire them.

- In Korea, the job-placement services in universities and colleges are in general staffed with graduates who have had little or no specific training for this work, apart from short in-service programmes.

*Specialist guidance training is beginning to be linked to HRD training.*

In a couple of countries, specialised career guidance training is becoming linked to human resource development (HRD) training. In the Netherlands, outside the basic in-service training for *schooldekanen*, the main training in career guidance is part of four-year HRD courses in five *hogescholen* (the third year being spent in a work placement). The notion is that all HRD staff should be trained in career guidance; it is also possible to specialise in career guidance in the final year. The courses can also be taken on a part-time basis. In Korea, there are plans to develop bachelor and master's degrees for staff in employment services, possibly linked to training for HRD roles.

An outcome of limited or inappropriate training arrangements is that many career guidance practitioners receive no thorough grounding in the basic theories of career guidance, little systematic exposure to the social and economic contexts and purposes of career guidance, and no systematic applied training in the techniques that form the basis of its practice. An example of a postgraduate course (at the University of East London) that attempts to ensure that comprehensive theoretical and practical training is provided is given in Box 7.1.

---

**Box 7.1. The Postgraduate Diploma in Careers Guidance at the University of East London**

The University of East London offers a Postgraduate Diploma in Careers Guidance that can be entered by those with a recognised university degree or equivalent. It can be completed either in one year full-time or in two to three years part-time. It trains people to work with a range of client groups. Successful completion can satisfy requirements for membership of the Institute of Careers Guidance (ICG). Students are required to build up a portfolio of evidence for this. The course covers:

**Guidance Theory and Practice:** Students learn the skills and processes of guidance interviews and group work, study a variety of theories relevant to guidance practice, and evaluate their implications for practice.

**Equal Opportunities:** Strategies to promote equal opportunities in a guidance context are taught, and awareness is raised of issues related to equal opportunities.

**Organisation Change and Development:** Students examine a guidance agency in the framework of organisation theory and change management. They acquire the skills needed to operate effectively and autonomously in a variety of contexts.

**Labour Market Studies:** Employment and training structures and labour market trends are studied. Students learn about and evaluate labour market information sources. Skills needed to operate at the interface of education, training and employment are acquired.

**Education Systems and Practice:** Contemporary education policy and the implications for career education are examined. Students acquire the knowledge and skills needed to take part in curriculum planning and implementation.

---

There is a strong case for increasing the level of career guidance training in a number of OECD countries. Career guidance has a substantial underpinning of theoretical knowledge, and its practitioners need to acquire a wide range of skills in order to do their job. There is a common core of knowledge and skills required by practitioners in all areas of career guidance. In addition, specialised knowledge and skills need to be acquired by those who work in specific areas: schools, tertiary education, employment settings and so on. This argues for extended periods of training in many countries, and higher levels of qualification.[2]

*Career guidance practitioners have limited capacity to influence occupational supply.*

Another of the criteria by which a profession can be distinguished from an occupation is the ability of its members to control, or substantially influence, occupational supply: for example by licensing; or by deregistration of those found guilty of malpractice. Few such procedures for controlling supply exist in the case of career guidance. There are, however, a limited number of exceptions. The most notable of these exists in Quebec, where strong licensing arrangements exist (see Box 7.2). In the United Kingdom, a weaker form of control is exercised by the Institute of Careers Guidance (ICG). The ICG, which represents career guidance practitioners, is the awarding body for the Qualification in Careers Guidance, one of the two principal qualifications required to work as a specialist career guidance practitioner in the major career guidance agencies in the United Kingdom. The ICG accredits the higher education institutions that provide the Qualification, and as such has a quality assurance role.

---

**Box 7.2. Professional regulation of career counsellors in Quebec**

In Canada (Quebec), anyone who wants to work as a guidance counsellor or career counsellor has to be a member of the *Ordre des Conseillers et des Conseillères en Orientation et des Psychoéducateurs et Psychoéducatrices du Québec* (OCCOPPQ).

The *ordre* has been in existence since 1963 and is one of 45 *ordres* which regulate a select number of professions in the province. Members have to possess a master's degree in guidance and counselling and submit themselves to periodic professional inspections.

---

*Some have established registers of guidance professionals.*

In some countries, registers have been established of career guidance practitioners:

- In Canada, in addition to the regulatory structures in Quebec, moves towards licensing career development practitioners are taking place in Alberta. In addition, the Canadian Counselling Association is seeking regulated status for the counsellors in a number of provinces and has introduced a "career development" category of membership, though its counselling orientation and its restriction to those with a relevant master's level qualification may limit its appeal.

---

2. However here are also dangers associated with inflated qualification levels: for example by requiring a postgraduate qualification at master's or doctoral level.

- In Germany, the German Association for Career Counselling (DVB) has established a Register of Career Counsellors which currently has 420 members (around 100 of these are not DVB members). To be registered, applicants have to demonstrate relevant initial qualifications, certified experience, and regular continuing training.

- In the Netherlands, a Careers Officers/Counsellors Register Foundation has been established by the Association of Vocational Guidance Counsellors (VBA).

- In Austria a professional association of counsellors, with a voluntary code of ethics, has been formed in order to attempt to raise the quality of career guidance provided by contractors to the Federal Employment Office.

- In the United States, licensing forms a significant part of the path to professionalisation: licensure is an important feature in 44 states (and the District of Columbia) (see: *www.counseling.org*). These regulations are linked with the quality assurance programme offered by the Council for Accreditation of Counselling and Related Educational Programmes (CACREP) (Plant, 2001).

*In many countries a range of associations represent career guidance practitioners.*

Alongside patchy training structures, there is also in many countries a very fragmented structure of representative associations, with different associations for those working in different sectors. In Canada, there are more than 20, and on some estimates as many as 40-50, associations representing career development practitioners. Many are at provincial level, operating in particular sectors, and sometimes even for different linguistic groups, each with different membership requirements. In Korea, there are at least four guidance associations: the Korea Vocational Counselling Association (mainly for vocational counsellors in the public employment services), the Korea Career Education Association (mainly for school counsellors and career education teachers), the Association of Job Information Centres at the Higher Education Level, and the Korea Career Counselling Society (mainly for people working in universities and in research institutes). Links between them appear to be limited. Such fragmentation is also an issue in Ireland, the Netherlands and Norway. This can make it difficult both for those who work in career guidance to see it as a whole, and for policy-makers to relate effectively to it.

*Some have developed federal structures to bring the different associations together.*

In a few countries, steps have been taken to bring together the different representative associations within a single structure. In Denmark, the eight separate national guidance associations are linked together beneath an umbrella organisation. In Australia, the Career Industry Consortium of Australia brings together all the major associations at both state and national level. In the United Kingdom, a Federation of Professional Associations in Guidance has been formed to bring the main associations together.

*Professionalisation can provide both benefits and problems for policy-makers.*

Professionalisation can have advantages in raising and maintaining the quality of services, and can play a role in helping to regulate markets for services. However a high degree of professionalisation, particularly when associated with an undifferentiated staffing structure, a weak knowledge base, inappropriate qualification requirements and traditional methods of service delivery, many of which exist in the case of career guidance, also poses problems for policy-makers. These problems can include increased costs and more expensive service delivery, limitations on access to employment in career guidance, an occupation that acts to protect its members more than the public, and difficulty in shaping and influencing service delivery within an enclosed system that resists external influences from public policy. The challenge for policy-makers is to strike a balance between the weak occupational structures and inadequate training arrangements that currently exist on the one hand, and the dangers of over-professionalisation that exist on the other.

## 7.3. Reshaping the career guidance workforce and its training and qualifications

*Occupational structures in career guidance need to be strengthened.*

*Creating clearer occupational structures*

Career guidance may not satisfy the standard criteria for a profession in most OECD countries, but neither in very many cases it is a clearly identifiable and separate occupation. It is a role, combined uneasily with many others. This is a stumbling block to the capacity of policy-makers to better use it to serve important public policy objectives. For example we have seen that where it is part of broader guidance roles, it is always accorded a low priority by those who are supposed to provide it. When it cannot readily be identified as a service that is available in its own right, people will continue to have difficulty in accessing it. And if it is not a separate occupational category, the problems of creating separate and appropriate training arrangements for it will persist. This has implications for the nature and quality of the career guidance services that policy-makers are able to deliver to citizens.

In order to increase access to career guidance throughout the lifespan and meet the needs of a wider range of clients, substantial changes are needed to the ways in which career guidance work is organised. A more differentiated workforce is needed, with wider use of trained support staff, and with career guidance practitioners acting as managers and co-ordinators of services, not just as personal service providers.

The priority for policy-makers in most OECD countries should be to create separate, and appropriate, occupational and organisational structures to deliver career guidance. Where such structures do not exist, policy-makers should consider intervening, for example in industrial tribunals, to have appropriate occupational classifications created, together with their associated qualification requirements. A model of a separate occupational structure, combined with a separate organisational structure, is provided later in Box 10.2.

## Strengthening training and qualification arrangements

*The nature and content of career guidance training is a major issue for policy-makers, influencing their capacity to provide appropriate services to diverse client groups.*

The level, content and structure of training courses, and the types of qualifications required of career guidance practitioners, have a major influence upon the types of career guidance services that governments are able to provide for their citizens. As an example, the absence of training at several levels makes it more difficult for governments to introduce differentiated workforces of the sort that make the United Kingdom's learndirect service (see Chapter 5) possible, or to introduce self-service methods. This has implications both for access to career guidance and for its cost. Wider use needs to be made of self-help techniques and of new technologies, and career guidance practitioners need to become accustomed to working in a wider range of settings. Lack of training in ICT- and telephone-based service delivery reduces the readiness of practitioners to adopt these methods, again with implications for access and costs. And the existence of separate training courses and qualification requirements for those providing career guidance in the different sectors of education and other settings, as occurs in Denmark, reduces the flexibility with which the career guidance workforce can be deployed as need and demand change. Yet government involvement in the training of career guidance workers is highly variable (see McCarthy, 2001), with purposeful intervention by policy-makers in training issues appearing to be the exception. Wide differences can be observed between countries in the extent to which governments directly provide either initial or recurrent training; in the extent to which they fund these; and in their involvement in setting the content of training.

All of this has major implications for the roles, skills and qualifications of those who work in career guidance. Addressing the level and content of career guidance training is thus a major issue for policy-makers. However in the face of these challenges:

> "For the most part, training is done the way it was 50 years ago. It is primarily talk-based, stemming from a psychological background (versus a career development or adult transition, or labour market background), and does not address the diverse career paths and complex labour markets that clients encounter. There is definitely a need for more diverse content in career development training programmes." (Hiebert, McCarthy and Repetto, 2002, p. 41).

*The level of training is insufficient in some countries...*

In many countries, deficiencies are evident in the quantity and level of training that is available:

- In Austria, there appears to be no specific training in career guidance available within tertiary education, and government in-service training is limited to quite short courses.

- In Norway, no formal tertiary-level training in career guidance is required of those who provide it either in schools or in the public employment service. In-service courses and experience are the principal training methods available.

- In Austria, the Czech Republic, Finland, Luxembourg and Spain, services that provide career guidance recruit psychologists, with no requirement that their degrees include specific training in the theories and methods of career guidance. In such circumstances work experience and in-service courses become the principal training methods.

- In Germany, despite the Federal Employment Service losing its previous monopoly, the main training provision currently available is that provided by the Service's *Fachhochschule* for its own staff. Few other courses are available in tertiary education institutions, although there are some moves to develop more.

*...and its content is deficient in a number of ways.*

There are also significant deficiencies in the content of career guidance training, in nearly all countries. Gaps and weaknesses noted by McCarthy (2001) include a lack of training:

- in the integration of technology, including ICT, into career guidance;

- that provides an understanding of labour market changes;

- that provides perspectives on transnational mobility. This is a particular issue within the European Union;

- in accountability issues and methods; and

- for support workers such as information officers and community liaison workers.

The OECD review has also made it clear that nearly all training programmes continue to concentrate upon the provision of career guidance as a personal, one-to-one service, focused upon immediate decision-making. Few programmes train practitioners to help people develop the skills to manage their own careers. Few try to develop the knowledge and skills required for designing and delivering curriculum-based career guidance. Even fewer try to develop the organisational, management and consultancy knowledge and skills required to deliver career guidance through the use of support workers and networks of community members. Furthermore, few try to provide comprehensive training that prepares people to provide career guidance in a wide range of settings (schools; tertiary education; the workplace; the community; employment offices) or to a diverse range of groups (young people as well as adults; the disadvantaged and those with special needs). And many, particularly those that are quite short, concentrate upon imparting knowledge. The strong skills-base of career guidance means that training programmes should both teach the necessary theoretical understanding, and develop a strong foundation of the skills required for practice.

*Existing training arrangements are a barrier to the implementation of key public policy objectives.*

Taken together, these gaps and weaknesses suggest that in many countries insufficient training, inappropriate training, or both, constitute significant barriers to the capacity of career guidance services to contribute to the implementation of lifelong learning and active labour market policies. Governments need, in many countries, to play a stronger role in raising the level and reshaping the content and structure of career guidance training arrangements.

*Comprehensive competency frameworks can be a first step in addressing training deficiencies.*

A first step in addressing these issues would be to develop comprehensive career guidance competency frameworks, of which the Canadian Standards and Guidelines for Career Development Practitioners (Box 7.3) represents one of the few available examples.[3] Such frameworks should describe the knowledge and skills required by career guidance practitioners at all levels, working in all sectors, and working with diverse types of clients. They can be used to construct qualifications, and training programmes to deliver these, at several levels, reflecting the needs of a differentiated workforce. Comprehensive competency frameworks allow qualifications and training programmes to be developed not only for full-time specialised career guidance practitioners, but also for those, such as career education teachers in schools, who are involved in career guidance for only part of their time, and for support staff such as information officers and community liaison staff.

Such frameworks allow a modular structure to be developed for training and qualifications. These contain a core of knowledge and skills to be acquired by all as well as optional elements reflecting needs in different settings and the needs of different types of clients. They can be used to develop standards for both initial training courses and qualifications, and recurrent training programmes. In the United States such standards have been developed by the Council for Accreditation of Counselling and Related Educational Programs to regulate and maintain the quality of the training career guidance staff. They incorporate a lengthy quality assurance process, including direct inspection of premises, the curriculum, and staff qualifications (Plant, 2001).

---

**Box 7.3. The development of a competency framework in Canada**

In Canada, the Standards and Guidelines for Career Development Practitioners provides a framework within which a variety of roles can be identified. It has been developed through a careful process of consultation and consensus-building.

The framework outlines a number of core competencies which all career development practitioners need to have, regardless of their employment setting. It also includes a range of specialised competencies, the need for which will vary according to the nature of the service being provided, the type of work setting, and the client groups that are being served.

The framework is being field-tested in a wide variety of settings to assess how it might be used. For further details, see Plant (2001) and *www.career-dev-guidelines.org*.

---

3.     The occupational standards of the United Kingdom's Employment National Training Organisation are another example, although these encompass not only guidance roles but also the fields of advice, counselling and psychotherapy.

*They also have advantages in the management of the career guidance workforce.*

Competency frameworks have a number of other advantages, in addition to bringing greater consistency and flexibility to training arrangements. They can help to provide clearer career paths for career guidance practitioners, including both vertical and horizontal progression,[4] and in particular more explicit recognition and progression for career guidance workers in support roles such as information officers. They have the potential to facilitate recognition and accreditation of prior experiential learning, as well as short courses and web-based learning, and to encourage continuous professional development.

---

4.  The review has revealed instances (for example in Denmark and Ireland) in which experience in specialist career guidance work in schools can be a route into management roles. This is likely to be due to the whole-school perspective and community liaison skills that are developed, in addition to the interpersonal skills required for the work

# CHAPTER 8. FUNDING CAREER GUIDANCE

This chapter outlines some of the problems involved in finding out how much governments spend on career guidance, and provides some partial estimates of this expenditure for a limited number of countries taking part in the OECD review. The chapter outlines some of the ways that governments fund career guidance, and discusses the implications of these methods for the nature and quality of services. In particular it discusses how consistency and quality may be assured in devolved funding systems and when services are contracted out. It concludes with a discussion of market models in career guidance, and of how governments might use them to widen access to career guidance.

The chapter's key policy conclusions are that:

♦ The information available on how much is spent on career guidance is very limited in nearly all countries. Such information is needed if policy-makers are to know what benefits they are getting in relation to costs. They need it to take into account the relative costs of different types of services, and of services to different types of clients, when they are planning how to deliver services.

♦ Sufficient, if incomplete, examples of cost and resource-use data are available from selected countries to allow it to be demonstrated that the problems involved in obtaining policy-relevant expenditure data are able to be solved.

♦ Within devolved funding systems, and when services are contracted out, questions arise about the residual responsibilities of central government, and about how the quality and consistency of services can be assured. Methods available to deal with the latter questions include staffing formulae, legislative requirements, performance contracts and student entitlements.

♦ A wider use of market models to fund career guidance services might allow government expenditure to be concentrated on those most in need, if those who could afford to pay were able and encouraged to do so. Reasonably strong markets seem to exist in a number of countries for career information, as well as for career guidance that is linked to outplacement services. However markets for personal career guidance have proven to be difficult to develop. Some of the reasons for this are inherent in the nature of personal career guidance. It has sizeable social benefits, as well as individual benefits; it is highly variable and thus hard to standardise and market on a large scale (unlike career information); and it is frequently not very transparent, with supply and demand both being hard to specify.

♦ Governments could assist markets in career guidance to grow through a number of steps: wider use of subcontracting as a way to finance services; helping to make the supply of and demand for services more transparent; linking career guidance to financing mechanisms such as individual learning accounts and training levies; and helping to set standards for the market in order to raise consumer confidence.

## 8.1. Estimating expenditure

*Information on how much is spent on career guidance is important for policy-makers...*

Information about expenditure on career guidance services is important to policy-makers for a number of reasons. They need to know whether benefits are commensurate with costs (assuming, of course, that benefit data is also available). Expenditure data is needed to know the relative costs of different types of services, or what is being spent to meet the needs of different types of clients. And it is important in making decisions about relative priorities: between both service types and client groups. Good data on the costs of different types of career guidance services and different types of delivery methods is also essential if policy-makers are to estimate what the costs might be, under different types of policy assumptions, of developing career guidance services that are universally accessible, throughout life.

*...but in all countries it is difficult to obtain.*

Not surprisingly, major problems exist in estimating how much governments, and other parties, spend upon career guidance. In the case of individuals and enterprises expenditure data is, to all intents and purposes, completely absent in all countries. Estimating government expenditure on career guidance also poses major difficulties, but not all of these are insurmountable.

*Some problems stem from the nature of the career guidance workforce.*

Some of the problems involved in estimating government expenditure stem from the nature of the career guidance workforce. This is difficult to identify when it is spread over many different government portfolios, at different levels of government, and when many of those who provide career guidance perform other roles as well. Given that staffing is the major resource involved in career guidance, problems in measuring staffing levels accurately will result in problems in measuring expenditure.

*Others stem from the ways that government services are funded...*

The problem of measuring real career guidance staffing levels interacts with the ways that some of the government services that provide career guidance are funded. While public employment services are normally funded directly by central government, this is less commonly the case in education portfolios. In the Netherlands, for example, virtually all education funds go directly to individual institutions, which then decide what they will spend them upon. In Denmark, the funds used for much career guidance are provided to regional and local levels in the form of block grants for particular education sectors, and the allocation of these to career guidance can vary across and within sectors by local priority. Obtaining consolidated expenditure data is also difficult in federal systems of government such as Canada and Australia. In Australia, some organisations are reluctant to release some information of this type on the grounds of privacy, or for commercial-in-confidence reasons. In combination, a part-time workforce and devolved funding decisions can make much expenditure information very difficult to track down.

*...from budgetary and accounting methods...*

How government budget data is published, and government accounting procedures, can also make it difficult to monitor expenditure on career guidance. This is particularly so where career guidance does not constitute a separate line-item in government budgets. However it can be an issue even where there are separate and identifiable services that provide career guidance, as in Luxembourg. It has been a problem even in Germany's Federal Employment Service, where a very large and specialised career guidance workforce exists: accounting methods there are currently being changed to allow career guidance expenditure to be monitored. Spain was able to provide data on salary costs for education information centres, but not for their operating costs which are included in general budgets.

Expenditure and resource-use data is easier to obtain where governments fund separate and specialised career guidance services, such as Careers Wales in the United Kingdom. Where such services are asked to assume additional roles, as in England's Connexions service which provides a range of youth services in addition to career guidance, specific expenditure data becomes harder to obtain.

*...from it having a low political priority, or from a lack of overall co-ordination of career guidance.*

As with measuring the size of the career guidance workforce, some of the problems in measuring expenditure stem from the fact that in some countries policy-makers have, to date, either not seen it to be important, or have lacked the necessary means to gather data in a co-ordinated way. Thus the Czech Republic, in its national questionnaire for the OECD review, commented that "This information is not monitored in the Czech Republic." And Luxembourg pointed out that problems in how its budget data is reported were added to by the lack, at the time, of any overall national co-ordination of career guidance.

Table 8.1. **Estimated average staff inputs in some Danish guidance services**

| Guidance service | Average annual guidance hours per student |
|---|---|
| Youth guidance | 0.9 |
| General adult education | 1.5 |
| Youth boarding schools | 1.8 |
| General upper secondary courses | 3.0-5.0 |
| Commercial colleges | 3.5 |
| Upper secondary education | 3.7 |
| Technical colleges | 4.9 |
| Agricultural schools | 7.0 |

*Nonetheless, examples exist of helpful resource-use data.*

Not all of these problems, however, are insurmountable. Finland, for example, reported that estimates of unit costs in the public employment service can be based upon the percentage of staff time spent on counselling. And Denmark provided (see Table 8.1) detailed estimates of resource use in different sectors of education based upon the average number of guidance hours received by students each year. When multiplied by average salary costs (not, in themselves, easy to estimate in Denmark) this can give an estimate of expenditure. However for many policy purposes resource data based upon average staff hours is very useful. Information such as that in Table 8.1, for example, could be used to estimate the likely cost, in terms either of expenditure or numbers of staff needed, of introducing an individual entitlement to career guidance. Or it could be used to ask questions about the fairness of and reasons for differences in resource use between different guidance services: the Danish data shows resources per student to be nearly eight times higher in the best-resourced service than in the worst-resourced.

The provision of data such as this requires career guidance staff to keep a record of their time use. Instances were encountered during the career guidance review – for example in Ireland's schools – of a reluctance by career guidance staff to do so on the grounds of "privacy". Such problems should be able to be resolved by policy-makers working with career guidance practitioners. In Ireland, for example, client record data is kept in adult guidance services to allow the implementation of policy goals to be monitored, as it is in adult guidance partnerships in England.

*Most countries can at best provide partial data.*

Some countries have not been able to resolve such problems, or perhaps have yet to begin to address them, and were able to provide little useful data on government expenditure. In other cases expenditure data was available for some sectors or services, but not sufficient to allow an estimate to be made of overall government expenditure on career guidance. Finland, for example, was able to provide detailed data on expenditure on career information and resource materials by the National Board of Education, but not on career guidance services in schools.

*A few are able to provide data from which estimates of overall expenditure on career guidance can be calculated, even if these are far from perfect.*

Despite problems such as those outlined above, three countries – Australia, Austria, and England – were able to provide sufficient data to enable at least a partial estimate to be made of overall expenditure on career guidance, and for this to be translated into an indicator of annual expenditure on career guidance per head of population aged 15-64. The three estimates are not directly comparable. Each, in its own way, is incomplete, and an underestimate of total expenditure. For Australia and England, for example, no information is available on direct career guidance services provided to the clients of public employment services, although some data is available on the cost of central career information services. For Austria, information is available on some career guidance services that are contracted out to other agencies by the public employment service, but not on the cost of career guidance directly provided by the service itself. Information on the expenditure elements included in, and absent from, each is given in Annex 4. The resulting estimates, which should be treated with a great deal of caution, show expenditure on career guidance per head of population aged 15-64 to be €11.48 in Australia, €8.48 in Austria, and €23.54 in England. Intuitively these orders of magnitude make sense in view of the intensity and level of career guidance services reported in national questionnaires and observed during national visits. They also make sense when the highest and lowest estimates are compared. In Austria's schools, part-time student advisers receive only 1-2 hours per week for their work, career education lessons are concentrated in grades 7 and 8, are often not given by careers specialists, and no external services provide systematic and specialised support for schools' career guidance programmes. In England, on the other hand, all schools must have a comprehensive careers library and must provide career guidance for the 13-19 year-olds age range, and an extensive external agency (Connexions) provides personal career guidance support to schools and colleges. In Australia the level of provision in schools falls between these extremes, being strong in parts of the country, and weaker in others. Similar degrees of difference between the three countries exist in other sectors. In the United Kingdom career guidance is stronger both for adults and in tertiary education than it is in Austria.

The three estimates of expenditure on career guidance per head of population aged 15-64 are liable to be incomplete, for reasons set out in Annex 4, or to be less than completely reliable through the inclusion of estimated rather than actual expenditure for some items. Nevertheless they represent a significant advance on previous knowledge. Hopefully, more detailed work will enable them to be refined and extended to other countries.

*The ingredients approach could be used by policy-makers to obtain better and more useful expenditure data.*

For some policy purposes, estimates of total expenditure on career guidance services, either across all sectors or within particular sectors, are important. For other policy purposes, however, estimates of the relative costs of providing different types of services, or of providing services to different types of clients, are needed. Problems in estimating levels of resource use across different types of services are not limited to the field of career guidance. It is common, for example in many areas of education, to find that official budget information is of limited value, and that expenditure decisions are taken at several different levels, or across several portfolios. Many of these problems can be addressed by the use of a systematic approach to the evaluation of cost-effectiveness. Specifically, the ingredients approach (Levin, 1983) offers a well-tested approach that has the potential to substantially improve policy-makers' understanding of the real resource demands of different types of career guidance programmes.

The ingredients approach involves a careful assessment of the actual ingredients used to provide a service (staff time, resource materials and capital costs for example) at the point of service delivery (in a school, in a community agency providing career guidance, in an employment office for example) and the estimation of their actual costs. When applied across a sample of the different settings in which career guidance is provided, it has the potential to illustrate not only what the key components of career guidance delivery costs are, but also how these costs vary according to the type of service being provided. Together with measures of outcomes or benefits, the ingredients method allows estimates to be provided of the cost per unit of effectiveness. It is particularly well suited to the estimation of costs under the types of circumstances in which career guidance is delivered in many OECD countries, and it deserves to be more widely adopted.

## 8.2.    Government funding: methods and issues

*Most career guidance is funded by governments...*

In most countries, governments provide the overwhelming majority of funds for career guidance: only some limited services are funded directly by individuals or employers.[1] The main alternative funding method exists in Germany, where the extensive career guidance services of the Federal Employment Office are, like its other services, funded by individuals and employers through the social insurance system.[2]

*...using a range of methods, which can affect the nature and quality of services.*

A range of government funding methods for career guidance exist. Funds can be provided by national governments: this is most commonly the case in public employment services. Or they can be provided by governments at the regional or local level, as is more often the case in school career guidance services. These differences are commonly associated with differences in the ways that funds for career guidance are managed. They can either be managed directly by central government, delegated to a government agency (as in the case of many public employment services), devolved directly to local-level institutions such as schools, devolved indirectly through a lower level of government, or subcontracted to community or other organisations. Often funds for career guidance form part of block grants for wider purposes, as in most career guidance within educational institutions in Denmark, and funds for wider youth support programmes in England's Connexions service. At times they are specifically earmarked for career guidance, as in funds provided to the *service d'orientation professionelle de l'administration de l'emploi* in Luxembourg. These different funding methods can affect the nature and quality of services, and so give rise to a number of policy issues.

*Devolution of funding decisions raises issues about residual national responsibilities and strategic co-ordination.*

### Issues in devolved funding systems

In many countries educational funding, especially for primary and secondary education, is devolved largely to regions or municipalities. Devolution to lower levels of government can also be observed in some countries' labour portfolios. Thus in Canada seven of the provinces have taken full responsibility for career development and other employment services, and have struck labour market development agreements with the federal government through Human Resources Development Canada (HRDC). In another five provinces these services are partly devolved. A

---

1.      And some services are indirectly funded by individuals, either wholly or partly, as in the case of students at private schools or colleges where student fees meet part or all of the costs of career guidance services.

2.      A similar example can be found in Austria, where the contributions that individuals and employers make to employees' and employers' Chambers contribute to the costs of services provided by those organisations.

similar situation exists in Spain's public employment service, with the autonomous regions in most cases taking full responsibility for employment services, including associated career guidance.

Such devolution raises the question of whether some career guidance responsibilities should be retained at the national level. In Canada, HRDC retains responsibility for national labour market information and for certain special programmes (notably for young people, for Aboriginals, and for people with disabilities). In Spain, the National Institute for Employment (INEM) retains a central, national occupational observatory, although some of the autonomous communities have their own occupational observatories, and common standards in some instances have yet to be developed. There is also an issue about whether there should be a national mechanism for strategic co-ordination. In Canada, overall strategic co-ordination of labour market matters between federal and provincial governments, including consideration of career guidance issues, is managed through the Forum of Labour Market Ministers. Similar arrangements exist in Spain.

Devolution of funding decisions also requires policy-makers and service managers to consider how they can ensure that there is minimal variation in the nature and level of services. For example some managers of educational institutions may see career guidance as being very important for the institution and its students; some may not. This issue is particularly likely to arise in countries where the performance of institutions is judged by the number of students that they recruit (inputs) or by output measures such as examination results, rather than by process measures or by longer-term outcome measures. This raises the issue of whether central government has a responsibility to ensure the consistency and quality of career guidance provision, and if so, how. Career guidance services in tertiary education are a particular case of this issue, because here central government control over how funds are used is weak in the face of traditional institutional autonomy. But it can also be seen in the case of school career guidance services, as both English and Irish research demonstrates (Morris, Rickinson and Davies, 2001; National Centre for Guidance in Education, 2001).

***Staffing formulas are one solution to this.***

Where funding to regions or to institutions takes the form of block grants, some central governments have imposed a *de facto* earmarking of funds for career guidance through the use of staffing formulas. This can be found particularly in the case of educational institutions. In Australia, the state of New South Wales makes formal provision for a staffing allocation of a full-time-equivalent careers adviser in each secondary school; in the Canadian province of British Columbia there must be a school counsellor for every 693 students in grades K-12; in Norway, guidance counsellors have a reduced teaching load according to a formula under a collective agreement which provides for a minimum of one hour per week per 25 students.

*Other solutions include legislative requirements...*

Central governments have also tried to make sure that devolution leads to career guidance actually being provided by using legislation. Often these requirements are fairly vague, and it is left to those who manage institutions to decide how to interpret and implement them. For example, 1997 English legislation requires each school to provide a minimum programme of career guidance, and to provide a careers library. And 1998 Irish legislation requires that "students have access to appropriate guidance to assist them in their educational and career choices". In each country, school inspectorates report on how legislative provisions are implemented. This may be complemented by research, such as that cited above.

*...and performance contracts.*

An additional approach, noted in Chapter 3 in the case of Finnish tertiary institutions, is for the annual financial contracts between the central government and universities to require plans for the improvement and promotion of guidance services.

*Student entitlements might be an alternative approach to ensure the consistency and quality of career guidance in devolved systems.*

Student entitlements to career guidance could be another way to ensure the consistency and quality of career guidance in devolved systems. Where they are considered, entitlements need to take into account the arguments in favour of diverse delivery methods raised in Chapter 5. In other words, they should not presume an entitlement to a certain number of hours of face-to-face personal career guidance, or of guidance practitioner time per student. If they were to be phrased in these terms, they would limit the incentive to provide more cost-effective services such as curriculum provision, group guidance, self-help services or ICT-based services. Framing entitlements around outcomes rather than inputs might be one way to achieve this flexibility. So might mandated requirements for career guidance to be included in school planning, together with appropriate accountability requirements. However they are framed and monitored, if student entitlements to career guidance provision are to be introduced in a financially responsible way, they need to be supported by the type of expenditure data discussed in the previous section.

*Some career guidance services are contracted out in a number of countries, and for a number of different reasons.*

### Contracting out

In a number of countries, governments have contracted out some of their career guidance services. This occurs for a number of reasons. Often it is based upon the view that the role of government is to purchase services and to assure their quality rather than to provide them directly. Services are also contracted out because they are cheaper, as staff in contracted agencies tend to have lower salaries and fewer benefits than civil servants.[3] This can make it easier to argue for additional resources to extend services. In addition, subcontracted services are at times felt to be more flexible in responding to changing demands. As noted in Chapter 4, community-based and private organisations are often felt to be more attuned than government organisations to the distinctive needs of certain client groups or to local

---

3.    In services contracted out by the federal government in Canada, salaries are about 10% less, and employment-related expenses amount to an additional 12% of salary compared to 25% among government employees.

labour market circumstances. Contracting out can occur within highly devolved financing systems, with minimal central government involvement, and also where central governments retain quite detailed supervision of the conditions under which services are provided.

In some cases contracting out of career guidance services has been part of a wider contracting out of employment services, but it has also taken place in other contexts.

*In Australia*, where the entire public employment system was contracted out in the mid- to late 1990s (OECD, 2001d), the national questionnaire refers to a 1996 review which showed that very few providers of case management services directly included career guidance. Those employment service clients who need specialised career guidance services are referred to CRS Australia, a separate organisation that has been subcontracted to provide the Career Counselling Programme. Subcontracting is also used to deliver the Jobs Pathway Programme which provides a range of locally-based support services to school leavers: these services may include some career guidance.

*In Austria*, the Federal Employment Office contracts out some guidance services to a range of for-profit and not-for-profit organisations which in turn can contract services to private counsellors. Much of this work takes the form of six-week orientation courses for groups of 14-20 people, which cover matters such as job finding techniques and career planning, but also personal and social skills. In an attempt to develop an improved approach to quality assurance, and in particular to help ensure the standards of the staff providing the services, a Professional Association of Counsellors was formed in 2001.

*In the Netherlands*, the Centres for Work and Income provide initial one-stop centres for benefit claimants. The services that they offer include basic information on career guidance. Those who are eligible for more intensive employment reintegration services, which may include some career guidance, are then channelled via the municipalities or the Employers' Insurance Benefits Agency to private-sector reintegration companies from whom these services are purchased. However the choice of provider is made by the official authorities, rather than by clients. This has led to a complex and cumbersome system, which seems likely to have increased bureaucracy rather than reducing it (see Box 8.1).

*Also in the Netherlands*, there has been a progressive privatisation of state-funded guidance offices which previously had worked with schools (see Chapter 3). After consolidation into 16 regional guidance offices (AOBs), their funds were progressively passed to schools, which were free to buy services from the AOBs or elsewhere, or to retain the monies and provide the services themselves. Many schools preferred the latter course, partly because it enabled them to control the content of the guidance given. This meant that many of the AOBs disappeared. As in the case of the reintegration services, the power to purchase career guidance services was placed not in the hands of individuals, but in the hands of institutions with their own agendas and priorities.

*In England* the government has established a national network of regionally-based partnerships to provide career guidance to adults (see Chapter 4). These services are provided under contract to the central government, through the Learning and Skills Council.

---

**Box 8.1. Subcontracted private reintegration services in the Netherlands**

In the Netherlands, the Centres for Work and Income (CWI) screen those eligible for social-security benefits for access to employment reintegration services. The purchase of these services is carried out at a second level: by the Employers' Insurance Benefits Agency, or by the municipalities. They award annual contracts to private reintegration agencies, with quality, outcome and price as important criteria. Some of the work of the reintegration agencies is contracted on to sub-contractors (or even sub-sub-contractors), so adding further levels to the process. Sub-contractors complain about the number of clients who fail to turn up for appointments, because of the complex process and delays in receiving information on appointments.

There is concern in the Netherlands about quality assurance in this process. It has resulted in a separation between the diagnosis of client need at the CWI, the selection of the provider, and service provision. Case management occurs at the second level, but is largely a series of paper transactions: direct contact with clients is concentrated at the other two levels. One way to reduce the complexity might be to place the purchasing power in clients' hands. Some moves in this direction have already been made.

---

*Contracting out can have different consequences for quality.*

The above examples suggest that contracting out can be associated with different consequences for quality. One is the risk, commonly associated with monopsonies (a single purchaser associated with multiple suppliers of services), that competition between service providers results in price and quality both being driven downwards. There are suggestions in the above Austrian example that this might have occurred. Another is the type of complexity, and separation of purchase and supply, that has occurred in the Netherlands. Subcontracting can also, within a devolved system, as illustrated by the example of career guidance in schools in the Netherlands, lead to the erosion of services. On the other hand the English example illustrates that subcontracting can be associated with the imposition of strong quality standards. As pointed out in Chapter 4, adult guidance partnerships in that country must adhere to national career guidance quality standards in order to receive government funds. The Australian Career Counselling Programme is another example of a contracted service in which strong quality standards have been applied. The issue of quality in career guidance, and of the means by which it can be assured, is taken up in Chapter 9.

## 8.3. Market models

*There are two reasonably strong markets in the career guidance field:...*

A number of private markets exist for career guidance and information services. There are two areas in particular where markets are reasonably vibrant. These are the publication of career information and other career materials; and outplacement agencies, which commonly include impartial career counselling, independent of the interests of particular firms or particular educational institutions. A substantial private market, including an on-line market, also exists for employment agencies, although these generally offer only limited career guidance services.

*...in career information...*

The important role played by the private sector in producing career information has already been discussed in Chapter 6. As noted there, many publications, videos, CD-ROMs and web-based products are produced by private companies. These are funded by charges to consumers, by advertising, by government, or by a mix of these. In addition to career information, these privately published resources include self-help manuals and career education materials. Most of this market is unregulated, apart from voluntary guidelines. In a few cases, however, education authorities may review and identify selected career education materials as approved learning resources to be used with the official curriculum: this is the case in Canada (British Columbia), for example.

Markets for career information and other published resources exist for a number of reasons. Foremost among these is the high value that people place upon information as a basis for informed and satisfying decisions. In career guidance, as in other markets, information is a valued commodity. Other factors include the relatively low unit cost with which career information can be produced, compared to other career guidance services such as personal interviews; and the ease, again compared to personal interviews, with which these products can be distributed in a standardized form to a mass market.

*...and in outplacement agencies.*

A further area where a well-developed market exists is outplacement agencies. In Australia, for example, it is estimated that there are some 250 agencies of this kind. These agencies commonly include career counselling, and the fees are normally paid not by the individual end-users but by their employers. A Spanish example of such an outplacement service is given in Chapter 1.

Outplacement is, perhaps, the one area where employers are prepared to pay for genuinely impartial career counselling, since their concern is to help the employee's decision-making so that they leave in a positive way. In such cases employers have little interest in the content of the client's decision, unlike the cases in which they provide career guidance for reasons of internal career development for employees that they want to keep. Sometimes these schemes are confined to professional or managerial employees; sometimes they are applied more broadly.

There may be government subsidies for outplacement services. In Korea, for instance, government subsidies can cover half of the costs in the case of small- and medium-sized organisations, and one-third in the case of large organisations.

The market for outplacement services tends to be volatile, linked to the economic cycle: it is much stronger in times of recession, when companies are laying off staff, than in times of economic growth. Some providers attempt to compensate for this by offering consultancy support to the construction and operation of career development systems within companies.

*A strong market also exists in employment agencies...*

In the case of employment agencies, a substantial market has developed in many countries such as Korea, where there were 3 592 for-profit employment agencies registered in 2002. There has also been growth of private agencies in a number of countries where placement services were formerly a public monopoly, such as Denmark, Germany and Norway.

*...although career guidance services as part of them are generally limited.*

In general, such placement agencies offer only limited elements of career counselling.[4] Where such services are charged to individuals, conflicts of interest can arise. An example is consultants being paid by a current employer to give career counselling to someone being made redundant, and being paid a second fee by a new employer for "headhunting" the same person (Gurney *et al.*, 2000). In Germany, there are regulations that payment for career counselling can only be accepted from individuals where the service is not also providing a placement service, on the grounds that employer payments for the placement service might compromise the counselling process.

*Some countries also have limited markets for career guidance paid for by individuals.*

In some countries there is also a limited market for career guidance services paid for by individuals. Information on the extent of this market is sparse, although some countries are able to provide data.

*In Australia*, it is estimated that there are around 600 individuals and organisations offering career guidance. Many also provide services to organisations. Those working in sole practice report that it is difficult to earn a full-time living from the fees that they are able to charge.

*In Canada*, there are a number of private practitioners who specialise in career guidance or offer it as one of a range of counselling and consultancy services (assessments for insurance compensation in injury and accident cases can be a lucrative sideline). There are some signs that the private sector may be increasing, driven in part by parents' awareness of the deficiencies of career guidance within the public school system. There is also a growth of interest in career coaching. This may involve coaching in job-search skills or it may involve a more long-term supportive relationship (usually for senior executives, paid for by their employers). On the other hand, the growth of self-help materials, on-line information, and career development programmes in high schools may be having a negative impact on the potential for this market to grow.

*In Germany*, the Federal Employment Service's former monopoly both of placement and of vocational guidance services ended only in 1998.[5] The private sector ranges from individuals working by themselves to large consultancy companies offering outplacement and career-development

---

4.  Web-based services are, however, increasingly offering "guidance" or "careers advice" as a "loss leader" (Offer *et al.*, 2001).

5.  Some private services already existed prior to 1998: a judgement of the European Court of Justice in 1991 had ruled that the service's monopoly of placement services constituted an inadmissible restriction on the placement of senior executives and managers by private human resource consultants.

services, often as part of a wider range of services. The German Association of Management Consultants (BDU) has around 10 000 members, some 20% of whom claim to provide some career counselling services (though no information is available on how much of their time this consumes). The telephone yellow pages list some 630 individuals and organisations under the title *Karriereberatung*. Of the 420 current members of the Register of Career Counsellors set up by the German Association for Career Counselling, 35 are from the private sector. It is unclear to what extent these various services derive their income for career guidance services from individuals, from employers, or from public bodies like the Federal Employment Service and the municipalities.

*In the Netherlands*, a fairly substantial private sector in career guidance provision has developed. It includes the surviving regional guidance offices (AOBs), companies formed by staff from the AOBs or from the former public employment service, some sole traders from these and other backgrounds, and a range of other organisations including some large consultancy organisations. Some of these providers concentrate on offering career guidance. Others offer it as part of a range of other training and HRD services. No information is available about the number of people who pay directly for such services or about how much they pay. It seems likely, however, that this part of the market is very limited: figures reported by the former AOBs on the proportion of their turnover generated from private customers fluctuate between one per cent and five per cent (Meijers, 2001).

*In Norway*, a fairly new feature of the guidance system has been the emergence of a small private sector. The first and largest of these agencies was set up in 1990 and currently has five offices and five employees in different parts of the country. A further four small agencies have been set up since then. They tend to make more extensive use of psychometric tests than most other guidance services do. A recent Norwegian initiative to improve the co-ordination of career guidance services is to focus in part on how the role of private providers might be extended (see Section 9.1).

*Individuals seem reluctant to pay for career guidance at full-cost rates.*

In general, individuals appear to be reluctant to pay for career guidance – or at least reluctant to pay at full-cost rather than marginal-cost rates. This is a policy issue, given the limited nature of services available to adults in most countries (see Chapter 4). It may be only a transitional problem, based on the fact that users have been accustomed to such services being free of charge and that it takes time for them to adapt to market-based provision. However it could be a systemic problem, based on the difficulties of treating career guidance as a commodity in the ways a market would require (Watts, 2001).

*For this and other reasons, guidance is difficult to manage on a market basis.*

There are several reasons why career guidance is hard to handle through private markets (Grubb, 2002b). These include the fact that both supply and demand are difficult to specify and define, with even those who provide services often not able to agree on how to describe the services they offer. In addition, career guidance is highly variable in nature, and is often subsumed within other services such as education and job placement. For some needs, acceptable alternatives such as self-help tools on web sites are available free of charge. Also, there are large societal benefits that flow from career guidance, as outlined in Chapters 1 and 2. This suggests that if it is not only individuals, but also the wider society, that benefits from career guidance, it is harder, compared to other goods and services, to place most of the costs upon the individual. And, as discussed above, personal interviews, which to date have been the main delivery method of career guidance, are hard to standardise and to associate with economies of scale. Finally, many of the individuals who most need personal career guidance are least able to afford to pay for it, and least likely to be willing to do so.

On the other hand, given arguments in favour of expanded provision of career guidance for adults, in particular, it can be argued that the wider adoption of market-based funding methods would allow those who can afford to pay to make a financial contribution towards the costs of the services that they need, and for government funds to be concentrated mainly upon those least able to pay. In general, services paid for by individuals or employers tend to be geared towards professional and executive levels; those purchased by public bodies tend to be geared to the unemployed or other disadvantaged groups (*i.e.* to be compensating for market failure). Thus governments have an interest in considering what steps they might take to encourage the wider use of private markets in the provision of career guidance.

*Policies to extend career guidance could seek to work in part through the market.*

The reality is that the market model represents the fallback position where there is a policy vacuum (Grubb, 2002b) – in the case of funding of guidance for employed adults, for example. In principle, however, policies that were based on an acceptance that career guidance is a private good as well as a public good could work at least in part through the market.[6] A comprehensive strategy for lifelong guidance for all could encourage both public and private funding. Thus, in Australia, a House of Representatives Standing Committee inquiry on mature-age workers recommended that the government should "fund a universal, professional careers guidance service, available without fees to young people at school, and to all job seekers on benefits". It further commented: "It is appropriate that adults not on benefit should pay for career guidance. A sliding scale of fees could be devised taking into consideration a client's circumstances" (House of Representatives Standing Committee on Employment, Education and Workplace Relations, 2000, pp. 135-137). Such a policy position has yet to be implemented in Australia. However it is an important example of how policy-makers might be able to think about ways to combine different types of funding models for different client groups in order to build career guidance systems that are universally accessible, throughout life.

---

6.      The substantial social benefits associated with career guidance which were outlined in Chapters 1 and 2 constitute a case for some government subsidy of such services, in addition to contributions by individuals, in order to make them more affordable. Public investment in career information which is available to both public and private providers is one form of such subsidy.

*This implies three roles for government.*

A mixed funding model, such as that suggested above, implies three roles for government:

- Stimulating the market in order to build its capacity.

- Regulating the market and assuring the quality of services, both to protect the public interest and to build consumer confidence.

- Compensating for market failure where this is appropriate.

*Subcontracting policies are one way of stimulating the market.*

One measure to stimulate the market and compensate for market failure is the subcontracting policies outlined above. For example in Australia the private career guidance sector has been given a considerable boost by government policies to contract out public services which are free to the user. Some of these, notably the Career Counselling Programme, concentrate upon career guidance. Others, including the Job Network and the Jobs Pathways Programme, may include career guidance among a wider range of education and employment services. In effect, successive governments have created a new industry in employment services, comprising a variety of providers in the public, private and voluntary sectors, which overlaps with the emerging career guidance industry. Many of these providers have tendered successfully for participation in a number of the government programmes: some specialise in this work; others incorporate it into a wider range of activities.

*So is a better specification of supply and demand...*

Another step that governments can take to help to stimulate private markets for career guidance is to improve the ways in which both supply and demand are specified. This could be by: separating career guidance from other services so that it has its own identity; creating clear, separate and readily identifiable training qualifications for those who provide career guidance; adopting and promoting quality standards for career guidance; commissioning consumer surveys of the need for and satisfaction with services; and strengthening the consumer voice in the provision of career guidance. Some of these are discussed further in Chapter 9.

*...the adoption of more innovative approaches to financing career guidance...*

Adopting more innovative approaches to financing career guidance is another way that governments can attempt to stimulate markets for it. Experiments with individual learning accounts have been launched in a number of OECD countries, including Belgium, the Netherlands and the United Kingdom. These encourage joint investment in learning by individuals, by employers and by the state. There are strong arguments in favour of such accounts being able to be used to purchase career guidance. As with other markets, appropriate information and advice can help to protect the value of investments in learning, and ensure that appropriate investment decisions are made. Knowing that people are more likely to make informed investment decisions is likely to encourage both employers and the state to invest in such schemes, as well as individuals. Van Wiele (2003) describes a learning and development account project in the Flemish Community of Belgium in which career guidance costs are accepted as allowable costs, alongside direct education and training costs.

Other mechanisms to encourage the co-financing of adult learning that are being experimented with in OECD countries include time accounts, interest rate subsidies, tax deductions and tax credits, income contingent loans, and transferable training loans (OECD, 2003c). Making career guidance an allowable expenditure item under training levies, as discussed in Chapter 4, is another way to finance career guidance that could encourage the growth of private markets. There seems merit in policy-makers exploring how these several mechanisms also might be used to encourage greater investment in career guidance by adults.

*...and setting standards for the market.*

Only a few limited attempts have been made to set standards for the market for career guidance:

- In Canada (Quebec), as outlined in Chapter 7, the titles of career counsellor and guidance counsellor are protected by law. Of the 2 183 individuals registered there in 2002, 27% were in private practice on a full-time or part-time basis.

- In Germany, the Federal Employment Service can prohibit private career guidance services from operating in order to protect the interests of clients. Career guidance practitioners who are expected to meet the interests of an employer or an institution must communicate this to their clients, indicating that it might influence the career guidance that is provided. And payment for career guidance can only be accepted from individuals where the service is not also providing a placement service. In practice, however, no control mechanisms seem to have been established to enforce these principles. The effect is that career guidance services in the private sector are effectively unregulated.

- In the United Kingdom (England), all career guidance services that receive public funds have to meet national quality standards. For other guidance services, however, these standards have only a voluntary status.

Other efforts to address the issue of quality standards are discussed in Chapter 9.

# CHAPTER 9. HOW CAN POLICY INFLUENCE THE PRACTICE OF CAREER GUIDANCE?

This chapter outlines some of the ways that policy can have a stronger impact upon the organisation and delivery of career guidance services. These include: improved strategic leadership and co-ordination; better use of evidence and data; the use of legislation; the development and promotion of quality standards; and the development of a stronger voice for consumers in shaping the nature of career guidance services. Many of these are weakly developed in OECD countries.

The chapter's key policy conclusions are that:

♦ Governments have an important role to play, in association with other stakeholders, in exercising strategic leadership so that career guidance services can be better planned and better co-ordinated. In many countries this role has not been exercised well, although some recent examples exist of more effective planning and co-ordination mechanisms that can encompass at least the key government portfolios.

♦ Better evidence and data are needed to improve policy-makers' capacity to steer their career guidance services. Governments can do a number of things to improve the evidence base for career guidance policy, including: improving administrative data (for example on the nature of career guidance clients, the types of services that they receive, and the costs of the services provided), working in association with career guidance representative organisations; and supporting, for example through funding programmes, the growth of expertise in policy-relevant research within the academic community.

♦ Legislation can be another instrument for steering career guidance services. However it is commonly quite general in nature. Its value as a steering instrument might be increased if it was more often used to define client entitlements.

♦ Service delivery standards are another instrument that can be used to steer career guidance services and enhance their quality, particularly if linked to funding. Standards that are developed specifically for career guidance need to be developed in association with career guidance practitioners. Outcome-focused quality standards are attractive within the context of lifelong learning and active employability policies.

♦ Governments should also strengthen the voice of consumers in the ways that services are delivered. Instruments include need and satisfaction surveys and community consultations.

## 9.1. Strategic leadership

*Governments have an important strategic leadership role, but need to exercise it in co-operation with other stakeholders.*

Governments have an important role to play in exercising strategic leadership and in co-ordinating career guidance services: both at the level of policy development, and in the delivery of services. But in many cases they do not manage all career guidance services directly, and even where they do, services require the support of partners of various kinds. So strategic leadership and co-ordination need to be carried out by governments in co-operation with other stakeholders. These include representatives of education and training providers, employers, trade unions, community agencies, students, parents, consumers, and career guidance practitioners (see Bezanson and Kellett, 2001). Such stakeholders need to be included not only in programme delivery, for example in some of the ways outlined in Chapter 3, but also more strategically, in providing advice and in helping to set the policy goals and frameworks for career guidance services.

*Leadership is needed so that career guidance can support lifelong learning policies.*

Clear strategic leadership, involving all key stakeholders, is needed to articulate a vision of how career guidance can support lifelong learning and sustained employability. It is needed: to clarify the role of different partners, including different career guidance services, translating such a vision into practical policies and programmes; to identify gaps in provision; and to determine how they can be filled.

*Strong co-operation is needed between education and employment portfolios...*

Within government, good co-ordination is needed between different ministries and agencies. In particular, there is in many cases a need for stronger co-operation between education and employment portfolios. Because career guidance supports people's pathways through learning and work, it needs to operate at the interface between the two. Where links between them are weak, gaps in services for those who do not fall neatly in one or the other can escape notice. Another risk is that services can be weakly resourced if neither portfolio sees them as their prime responsibility. Specific examples include services for early school leavers who are neither in the labour market nor in education, or for women wishing to return to work or learning after a period of absence. Another consequence of weak co-operation is that career guidance can become imbalanced: for example, as outlined in Chapter 3, concentrating upon educational choices without taking enough account of the employment consequences of these choices. In federal systems like those in Canada and Spain, where responsibilities are held at different jurisdictional levels, these problems of co-ordination and strategic leadership can be particularly difficult.

*...and is important for a number of specific operational tasks.*

There are a number of specific issues on which co-operation between the two portfolios is needed. An important one is the establishment of effective working links between schools and employment services to ensure that a strong labour market perspective is included both in personal advice provided to school students, and within curriculum-based career education programmes. This can have implications for the training provided to school-based career guidance staff, for schools' access to public employment service staff time, or both. Co-operation between the two portfolios is also needed to ensure that career information databases integrate information on education, training and employment. In Chapter 6 it was pointed out that the lack of such integration is a common weakness of career information systems. This can be avoided by better co-operation.

*Consultative bodies can be set up, which can also carry out tasks that need to be collectively owned.*

Mechanisms for involving stakeholders can include permanent bodies for consultation and advice on which stakeholders are represented. In addition to broad tasks such as setting strategic directions, identifying gaps in services, and co-ordinating what different stakeholders do, such bodies can be given operational responsibility for tasks for which high levels of co-operation and collective ownership are needed. Examples include: the development of quality standards; and the development of new frameworks for career guidance training and qualifications.

*Mechanisms for leadership and co-ordination are often quite weak.*

In many countries mechanisms that can provide such leadership and co-ordination for career guidance services, either within government or between government and other stakeholders, are inadequately developed. Policy objectives are often poorly defined, poorly articulated and poorly communicated within and across government portfolios. Forums in which government and non-government stakeholders can communicate and debate policy issues are frequently absent, both at national level and regionally or locally.

*However some countries do have such structures…*

A few examples exist of initiatives to provide strategic leadership and improved co-ordination for career guidance. In Norway, where the Directorate of Labour currently has a formal legal responsibility for co-ordinating career guidance, the public employment service (Aetat) has been given responsibility to set up a working group to propose ways to ensure national and local co-ordination of career guidance services, including the possibility of a permanent co-ordinating body. Its tasks includes considering how to provide career guidance for adults, and if and how private actors can be used as providers of services. Aetat has been asked to invite the relevant bodies to participate; among them are the Board of Education, the Norwegian Institute for Adult Education, the Career Centre at the University of Oslo, and the social partners.

In Luxembourg, the government has agreed to establish a mechanism to co-ordinate career guidance services. Its tasks are to include the development of a national strategy for lifelong guidance. Responsibility will be given to an existing tripartite committee on vocational training on which key ministries, as well as the social partners, are represented.

In England, the National Information Advice and Guidance Board has been set up to ensure coherence in planning career guidance services that are provided or funded by the Department for Education and Skills and the Department for Work and Pensions. Its purpose is to co-ordinate policy and provision both within and between the education and employment portfolios. Although it does not encompass all career guidance services (for example those in the private and not-for-profit sectors), it does encompass the largest and the most important of them. It is staffed by a secretariat located in the Department for Education and Skills. Also in the United Kingdom, the Guidance Council has been set up as an independent body. It includes representatives of the main stakeholder bodies, with government observers. It was contracted by the government to develop organisational quality standards.

*...and there is also potential to link to structures for developing lifelong learning strategies.*

In other countries, mechanisms exist that help to co-ordinate, or which have the potential to co-ordinate, national approaches to lifelong learning. For example in Germany, an Alliance for Jobs, Training and Competitiveness is developing a national lifelong learning strategy. It includes both of the relevant federal ministries – of education and of labour – as well as the social partners. In Korea, a high-level human resource development committee has been established which includes the Ministers of Education and Human Resources and of Labour. And in the Netherlands, structures are being developed between the Ministry of Economic Affairs, the Ministry of Education, Culture and Science, and the Ministry of Social Affairs and Employment, to co-ordinate policies on lifelong learning. For reasons discussed in Chapter 1, career guidance and its strategic leadership need to be key concerns for these structures.

*Stakeholder involvement can also be increased through broad public consultations.*

Other mechanisms to increase stakeholder involvement can include broad public consultations on needs and on the adequacy of services to meet these needs. For example in Canada (Quebec), the policy to develop the concept of the "guidance-oriented school" (*l'école orientante*) that was outlined in Chapter 3 stemmed from an extensive process of community consultation (the Estates General on Education). In the course of this consultation, the limitations of the previous career education provision – based on a programme taught largely by teachers who happened to have space in their timetables – were repeatedly pointed out, particularly by young people themselves. The criticisms were reinforced at a Quebec Youth Summit held in 2000.

## 9.2.   Evidence and data

*Policy-makers need a strong evidence base.*

Evidence and data are key tools, and tools of growing importance, for all policy-makers (Solesbury, 2001), including those responsible for career guidance policies and services. At the very least, strong and systematic evidence is needed to assess the match between career guidance services and policy objectives, but also to assess the need for new or expanded services, and the value that those who provide funds are getting for the funds invested.

*Career guidance has a strong research tradition, but this has had little relevance for policy.*

*Research*

Research is one of the ways in which the evidence and data needed for policy development can be gathered. Career guidance has a strong research tradition, but this has largely focused upon theories, tools and methodologies, and has less frequently been of direct policy relevance. Its focus upon outcomes, for example, has been weak, as outlined in Chapter 2, and its focus upon costs, as outlined in Chapter 8, even weaker.

*Policy-relevant research needs to focus upon outcomes.*

Research on the impact of career guidance has frequently been of limited help to policy-makers. In part this is because it is difficult research to do well: career guidance is often hard to observe directly, it is very diverse in nature, it is often embedded in other activities, and the outcomes it tries to achieve are diverse, diffuse and to some extent idiosyncratic to the needs of individuals. While much of the existing evidence is positive in nature, as outlined in Chapter 2, policy-makers have sometimes used the lack of hard evidence to support limited investment in services. Yet they have been reluctant to fund the complex, large-scale research that is needed to supply such evidence. There is certainly a need for more studies of the effects of specific kinds of interventions with specific target-groups. These should where possible include estimates of costs, so that cost-benefit analyses can be conducted. However there is also a need for a clearer specification of the outcomes expected from career guidance services and programmes. The Canadian Blueprint for Lifework Designs, described in Section 9.4 below, is a promising approach to this which sits well in a lifelong learning and active employability framework.

*Better evidence is also needed on inputs and processes.*

### Improved administrative data

Formal research is only one of the tools available to policy-makers to gather policy-relevant data. The collection of administrative data – for example on clients or on services provided – is equally important. Here, too, career guidance has been weak, as evidenced for example by the difficulty experienced by all countries in providing good data on the nature of the career guidance work force outlined in Chapter 7. Many had equal difficulty in providing data on career guidance clients. As an example, when asked about the information available on the extent to which career guidance services are used, Ireland replied that in the education sector "…there is little information available about the extent to which …services are used. There is no systematic recording of client and problem type, and no national standard for such records." Such a response was not unusual. The Netherlands replied that "there are only limited hard data on this subject".

In addition to an interest in the outcomes of career guidance, policy-makers need information to help them to understand its inputs and processes. Much of this can be collected through improved administrative data, as well as special surveys.[1] Information that is relevant for better understanding career guidance inputs and processes includes:

---

1.    It should be noted that the expansion of self-service and ICT-based techniques poses problems for the collection of this type of data that do not exist when services are provided through traditional face-to-face interviews in fixed service locations. With these newer types of service delivery, it is often difficult for service managers to know who clients are. Community-based surveys of the use of a range of service types, for example as a module attached to labour force surveys, are one way to address this issue. In some settings focus groups can be another method.

- The needs of different kinds of clients.

- The total numbers who receive career guidance and their characteristics (by age, gender, geographical region, socio-economic status, educational level, ethnic origin).

- The types of services received by different groups.

- Client satisfaction rates, and variations in these rates by client characteristics.

- The distribution of demands for services over time (hours of the day, days of the week, times of the year).

- The overall costs of services, and how these costs are shared between different parties.

- The relative costs of different types of services.

*A number of gaps are particularly evident.*

Four particular evidence gaps that were identified during the review were:

- The need within devolved school systems for more quantitative as well as qualitative information on the extent and nature of services provided. Such information was clearly lacking in Australia, Canada, Korea, the Netherlands and Norway, for example.

- The need for more information on the extent and nature of the private sector in career guidance provision, including who its clients are and how much they pay for what sorts of services. This gap is particularly significant if – as this report has argued it should be – such private provision is regarded as a matter of public concern.

- The need for more market research on people's career guidance needs and on where and how these needs are currently being met (for an example of such research, see MORI, 2001).

- The need for simple client monitoring procedures such as those described in Box 9.1.

---

**Box 9.1. Client monitoring in Ireland**

In Ireland, the new adult guidance pilots have developed a simple client recording instrument to allow the use of services by designated target groups to be monitored. In addition, the FÁS/LES Caseload Management System is used to monitor and track clients' progress.

Such experience has shown that it is possible to develop such an instrument in a way that preserves client confidentiality and that involves career guidance staff in a positive way in its use in order to improve service quality. There is a need to develop a similar instrument for use in schools. In addition to being an essential tool for policy-making, it would also be a valuable tool for individual guidance counsellors, giving them systematic rather than (as at present) impressionistic feedback on the services they provide. Feedback to individual institutions should be an essential feature in developing such an instrument.

---

*Some promising initiatives exist.*

To date, few OECD governments have systematically attempted to widen the knowledge base for career guidance through a comprehensive strategy that involves: improving administrative data; supporting the establishment of specialised career guidance research centres; directly commissioning programmes of relevant research and evaluation; and using all of these to improve policy and practice. There are, however, some examples of promising, if limited, initiatives. In Ireland a National Centre for Guidance in Education has been established, which, among other roles such as training, has conducted a number of policy-relevant surveys: for example on the extent of career guidance provision in secondary schools. In the Czech Republic the National Institute of Vocational Education has conducted extensive surveys on student use of and satisfaction with a range of career guidance services, both those provided within and by schools, those provided for schools by external agencies, sources such as the media and the Internet, and informal sources such as friends and family. In Denmark the Career Guidance Research Unit at the Danish Pedagogical University is being upgraded, and its focus widened to also encompass policy issues. And in Finland, an extensive and co-ordinated set of evaluations have been conducted of career guidance services in a number of sectors, with direct links to policy development (see Box 9.2).

---

**Box 9.2. A co-ordinated link between evaluation and policy development in Finland**

During 2000-2003 Finland conducted a wide-ranging evaluation of its guidance services: in comprehensive schools; in secondary education; in tertiary education; in adult education; and in the public employment service. While revealing many examples of good practice, a principal message from the evaluations was that national policies were fragmented, and that services have not been able to meet growing demand. Feedback mechanisms were found to be weak at the institutional level, and a need was revealed for stronger planning and leadership in guidance delivery (Kasurinen and Numminen, 2003).

The outcomes of the review process have been translated into policy in a number of ways. For example as outlined in Chapter 3, the variability in tertiary services that was revealed by the review has resulted in the relationship between funding and career guidance being tightened with institutions needing to prepare guidance plans as part of their performance contracts. Within schools, the National Board of Education will execute new national guidelines for guidance, and implement a web-based service to support the institutional self-evaluation of services. Additional initiatives have included the strengthening of in-service training for teachers and guidance practitioners, the creation of a network of regional consultants, the introduction of a number of regional pilot programmes, and the development of national standards for student-counsellor ratios.

In order to communicate and build upon the review process the Institute for Educational Research at the University of Jyväskylä, in co-operation with the Ministry of Education, the Ministry of Labour and the National Board of Education, hosted a national seminar on the future of career guidance in Finland in late 2002.

---

*However a more permanent infrastructure is needed to improve the evidence base.*

Many such examples, are however, largely one-off initiatives. In most countries, a stronger and more permanent infrastructure is needed for building a coherent body of evidence to underpin career guidance policy and practice. There are a number of concrete steps that governments can take to strengthen national data collection and research strategies in order to improve career guidance policy-making.

*This should encompass both improved data collection…*

Steps that can be taken to improve data collection include: the development of improved indicators on clients, services provided, staff time-use, costs and outcomes; and working with practitioner organisations and service providers to obtain agreement on consistent and improved administrative systems for data collection.

*…and the development of coherent research strategies.*

Steps that can be taken to improve policy-relevant research include: the creation of university chairs with a special focus on the link between career guidance and public policy; financial support for specialised national research centres within higher education; strengthening the role of higher education in the provision of career guidance training; the development of a body of expertise in policy-relevant research through the regular commissioning of policy-relevant research; and the development of a national research strategy on career guidance and public policy, in association with key stakeholders. The United Kingdom provides an example of a country that is moving in such a direction (see Box 9.3).

---

**Box 9.3. Developing a national research strategy for career guidance in the United Kingdom**

Compared to many other countries the United Kingdom has a strong knowledge base for its career guidance services. It has specialised centres for research and policy analysis in career guidance such as the National Institute for Careers Education and Counselling (NICEC) and the Centre for Guidance Studies at the University of Derby. In addition, several other centres both in tertiary education and outside it have research staff with a particular interest and expertise in career guidance. In the United Kingdom a high level of qualifications is required of career guidance practitioners. The role of the university sector in providing these qualifications is strong, including to postgraduate level. As a result, there is a group of academic staff with in-depth knowledge and expertise in the field of career guidance.

United Kingdom career guidance research is characterised by a focus upon policy and evaluation, not simply upon processes and techniques. The government frequently commissions research, uses it in policy development, and publishes it, even when its conclusions might be critical. This research is, in turn, used extensively by those who work in the field of career guidance, ensuring vigorous, healthy and informed debate between policy-makers and practitioners.

However much of the research that is conducted has been one-off and fragmented rather than strategic, and not disseminated widely or effectively. Following a conference jointly organised by the Guidance Council and the University of Derby Centre for Guidance Studies in May 2002 (The Guidance Council, 2002) a proposal to establish a National Research Forum for career guidance in the United Kingdom has been supported by the government. Initially there is to be a period of consultation and design, to be followed by a two-year pilot period. The key objectives of the Forum are to: develop a coherent research strategy relevant to policy and practice; help to identify research priorities and gaps; provide a co-ordinated approach to research to support investment in career guidance; and involve a wide range of stakeholders.

---

## 9.3.    Legislation

*The role of legislation varies…*

Countries vary widely in the extent to which legislation is used to steer career guidance services. It is not used at all as a direct steering device for career guidance services in Australia, and tends to be relatively weak and indirect in Korea and the Netherlands. However legislation on career guidance is extensive in Spain, and in Finland is regarded as a very important guarantee of service provision. In the United Kingdom legislation plays an important role, but alongside other steering methods.

In Canada rather than legislation, agreements between levels of government or between government departments, and personal service contracts between governments and non-government service providers are used to steer services.

*...but it tends to be general in nature.*

In most instances where legislation is used, it requires government institutions and agencies, such as schools or public employment services, to provide career guidance, but only in very broad terms. In Ireland, the Education Act requires schools to ensure that "students have access to appropriate guidance to assist them in their educational and career choices". The Labour Services Act requires the Irish Training and Employment Agency (FÁS) "to provide, or arrange for the provision of, whether for reward or otherwise, services consisting of the provision of guidance, advice and information in respect of choice of career and employment and to assist (whether financially or otherwise) in, and co-ordinate, the provision of such services by others". And in Norway, the Education Act states simply that: "The pupils have the right to necessary guidance on education, careers and social matters". What is "necessary" is largely left to schools to define. Denmark has had a separate Act on career guidance since the mid-1950s, and it was last revised in 1996. The legislation, however, simply provides an overall framework for services to be offered by educational institutions, public employment services, and other relevant authorities and agencies.

In some cases the main purpose of the legislation is to clarify jurisdictional responsibilities. For example in the United States, the Carl D. Perkins Vocational and Applied Technology Act of 1990 required that each state give assurances that it would provide leadership, supervision and resources for comprehensive career guidance and vocational counselling (see Bezanson and Kellett, 2001).

*Sometimes it is more specific.*

Sometimes legislation is more specific in indicating the types of services that are to be provided, and to whom. For example in Germany, the Framework Act for Higher Education requires institutions of higher education to "inform students and applicants on the opportunities and conditions of study and on the content, structure and requirements of study courses" and during the entire study period to "assist students by providing subject-oriented advice". In providing such guidance, it also requires institutions to co-operate with "the authorities responsible for vocational guidance". Legislation may also provide some specification about staffing. For example in the Netherlands, the Secondary Education Act states that "one or more members of the staff shall be assigned the task of careers teacher/co-ordinator". Legislation more rarely, however, specifies the quality standards that are to be used in service provision such as staff qualifications.

*It could be used more to define client entitlements.*

While legislation is commonly used to impose obligations for service provision, it is less frequently used to specify client entitlements. As a result, wide variation in the nature and quality of available services is observed, even where legislation requires career guidance to be provided.

The use of legislation to specify entitlements to career guidance, or to mandate processes for local accountability, might be ways, especially within devolved systems, of helping to ensure greater consistency in standards and quality.

## 9.4.    Quality standards

*Quality standards can cover not only career information and staff competencies but also service delivery.*

Quality standards can be developed for career information, for the qualifications that are required for employment as a career guidance practitioner, or for membership of relevant associations. The discussion here is confined to the use of quality standards as a way to influence how organisations deliver career guidance. Such standards can apply either to the processes used to deliver career guidance (the more common case), or to the outcomes expected from it.

*Such standards are particularly important in decentralised and market-based systems...*

Quality standards are particularly important in decentralised systems and in systems in which outsourcing is used extensively by governments to purchase services. Through links with funding, they can be a way for governments to try to ensure quality in such systems. For example in England, all adult guidance services that get public funds have to demonstrate that they conform to national career guidance quality standards (see Box 9.4). When private markets are used to deliver and fund services, quality standards can also be a way for governments to encourage individuals and employers to invest in career guidance.

*...but have a role in centralised systems too.*

A systematic approach to quality standards is also required in more centralised systems such as Austria and Germany. In such systems quality has often been presumed to be assured through administrative controls and through the specification of the qualifications required of staff. But this is too limited, particularly where staff qualifications are quite weak or variable. Other methods can be used to ensure quality within such systems. Examples include: performance targets, including targets for access to services by priority client groups; client monitoring and feedback mechanisms; and standards on issues such as impartiality.

*Standards can be of four kinds:...*

Service delivery standards can be of four types:

- Generic standards applied to a wide variety of activities, of which career guidance is only one.

- Standards developed for a particular sector (of education, for example) which includes guidance among its range of activities.

- Standards developed specifically for the career guidance field, with an accreditation procedure to enforce them.

- Voluntary guidelines developed for the career guidance field, which services can adopt and apply if they so wish.

*...generic standards...*    *Generic standards*

Generic standards include the ISO 9000/9001/9002/9003 quality models, the European Foundation of Quality Management standards, and the Total Quality Management standards. They are based on an industrial production model, but have been implemented in a small number of guidance services in Belgium, Denmark, Ireland and the Netherlands. They tend, however, to be seen by guidance practitioners as a top-down control mechanism rather than as a tool for improving how services are provided (Plant, 2001).

*...standards designed for specific sectors...*    *Standards designed for specific sectors*

Denmark provides an example of standards developed for a particular sector. There, in vocational education and training, guidance is included as an integral part of the quality-assurance processes for the institution as a whole. These are on a self-assessment basis, but with audit processes including spot checks to ensure that colleges are able to support what they claim.

In some such cases, however, the standards are not very specific about how career guidance should be provided. In the Netherlands, the inspections to which all state-funded educational institutions are subject are the main quality-assurance mechanism in guidance as in other areas. The inspectorate publishes a brief overall assessment based on these inspections in its annual report. The attention given to career information and guidance in the inspections seems to vary greatly. Much depends on whether there is anyone on the inspection team with an interest or some competence in the area. Where this is not the case, the treatment of career guidance seems often to be limited. The United Kingdom's Office for Standards in Education, which conducts inspections of schools and colleges, has specific criteria to be used for the inspection of career guidance programmes, and publishes separate reports on the outcomes of these inspections (see *www.ofsted.gov.uk/*).

---

**Box 9.4. The matrix quality standards in the United Kingdom**

In the United Kingdom, quality standards for career guidance delivery were initially developed by the Guidance Council, an independent organisation established in 1993 that represents career guidance organisations, and are now managed by the Employment National Training Organisation. The matrix standards, as they are known, cover five areas that directly concern the ways that individuals are helped (for example how effectively they are helped to explore options and make choices, or to gain access to information) and five areas that concern the ways that services are managed (for example how well they make use of client feedback, or develop their staffs' skills). Career guidance organisations wishing to be accredited by the United Kingdom's Guidance Accreditation Board are assessed against the matrix quality standards. For some funding purposes, organisations wishing to receive government funds must be accredited against the standards.

As well as being used for accreditation purposes, the standards can be used for quality improvement. Organisations that want to use them to improve the quality of their services can use consultants from a register maintained by the Employment National Training Organisation. Further details of the matrix standards can be obtained at *www.matrix-quality-standards.com*.

---

*...standards designed for career guidance...*

### Standards designed for career guidance

The main example of organisational quality standards developed specifically for the career guidance field, with an accreditation procedure to enforce them, is the standards developed by the Guidance Council in the United Kingdom. These are described in Box 9.4.

*...and voluntary guidelines.*

### Voluntary guidelines

Voluntary quality guidelines exist in a number of countries. In Australia, a Career Education Quality Framework for use in schools was developed by the Australian Student Traineeship Foundation and the Career Education Association of Victoria. Incentives for schools to use the framework have been provided by adopting it as the reporting basis for a National Innovation in School Careers Programmes Award. However because participation in the scheme is voluntary, it tends to be undertaken by schools which already have strong programmes. Thus its potential as a quality improvement tool is more limited. In Canada, some organisations have developed their own standards, sometimes with support from materials developed by such bodies as the Canadian Career Development Foundation, but this process is informal and lacks a clear implementation strategy.

In Denmark, following the publication of ethical guidelines in 1995 by the then National Council for Educational and Vocational Guidance, additional guidelines have been published for the development of quality-assurance processes. These suggest that each service should discuss and agree upon quality criteria and set up appropriate self-assessment procedures. In Ireland, guidelines for schools on guidance programme planning have been issued by the National Centre for Guidance in Education. In the United Kingdom, a number of voluntary quality frameworks for use in schools have been developed at local level. They do not have any formal national status, for example in relation to school inspections.

*How standards are developed will influence their effectiveness.*

The process used to develop standards is important. If there is a strong sense of ownership by stakeholders, including the services themselves, the standards are likely to be trusted and effective. This is why governments may seek to ask stakeholder representative bodies to develop the standards on their behalf. Whether or not they do so, they need to work in strong partnership with career guidance representative organisations, both in developing quality standards, and in developing the types of new qualification arrangements referred to in Chapter 7.

*Standards can be used to improve quality.*

In addition to providing assurance of quality to funding bodies and consumers, quality standards can be part of strategies for quality improvement. One way of doing this is for the standards to be supported by a consultancy service. If the standards are linked to an accreditation procedure, it is helpful if the consultancy service remains separate from this procedure (for an example of such separation, see Box 9.4).

*The impartiality of services is an important issue for quality standards.*

Quality standards that are designed for the delivery of career guidance should address the need for transparency about the neutrality and impartiality of career guidance, an issue which has been raised several times in this report. The United Kingdom matrix standards require that people have access to impartial and objective career guidance wherever possible, and that where it is not they be made aware of the purposes and limitations of the career guidance available. And in Germany, Social Code III states that career counsellors who are expected to meet the interests of an employer or an institution must communicate this to their clients, indicating that it might influence the counselling process.

*Career guidance quality standards can also focus upon outcomes, adopting a developmental perspective.*

*Standards that focus upon outcomes*

Career guidance quality standards can also focus upon outcomes, for example by specifying the types of skills and competencies that career guidance should try to achieve. The Canadian Blueprint for Lifework Designs is an important example of such an approach. Based upon a model originally developed in the United States by the National Occupational Information Coordinating Committee (1996), the Canadian Blueprint[2] was extensively piloted over a four-year period prior to implementation. It specifies ten broad competencies in three areas: personal management; learning and work exploration; and life/work building. Each is described at four levels, corresponding to developmental stages in people's lives. The Canadian model is currently being field tested in Australia (McMahon, Patton and Tatham, 2003).

*These are attractive in a lifelong learning and active employability context.*

Outcome-focused quality standards designed within a developmental perspective are particularly attractive in a lifelong learning and active employability context. At the least, they can be used as a framework to assist the design of career guidance tools, programmes and services. They have significant potential as a tool for policy-makers wishing to find ways to shift career guidance services from a focus upon the implementation of immediate, short-term decisions to a broader approach that also encompasses the development of career-management skills.

## 9.5. Strengthening the consumer voice

*Strengthening the voice of consumers on how services are provided is another lever that policy-makers can use.*

Policy-makers who wish to make career guidance services more responsive to the needs of clients can use a number of ways to strengthen the voice of consumers in determining how services are organised and provided. Focus groups and community consultations are one such method. An example is the use of such methods as a basis for the development of *l'école orientante* in Quebec, outlined in Section 9.1. Finland is another country in which extensive use has been made of student views in evaluating the effectiveness of career guidance services in education (see Box 9.2). This has been done both through student surveys and through the direct involvement of student unions in planning guidance services.

---

2.     Details can be obtained at *www.blueprint4life.ca.*

Client monitoring and satisfaction surveys, such as those conducted by the Czech National Institute for Vocational Education (see Section 9.2), and client entitlements, can be other important ways to strengthen the input that consumers have on the nature of career guidance services. The national quality standards used in the United Kingdom (see Section 9.4) presume that such methods will be used by career guidance services. In a related way, surveys of citizens' need and demand for services can be used for service planning: for example in determining the location and hours of operation of services, assessing relative needs between different client groups, and assessing the balance between different types of services that should be provided.

There is also a potential for career guidance services to be used to improve the responsiveness of educational institutions to consumer needs. This might be done by managers systematically using career guidance practitioners as intermediaries, either through advocacy on behalf of individual clients, or through general feedback mechanisms to service managers (Oakeshott, 1990). An Austrian example of such a systematic approach is given in Box 4.1. In Sweden, under an adult education initiative from 1997 to 2002, learners were not permitted to start an education or training programme without first seeing a guidance counsellor and drawing up a learning plan: funding followed the learner, but only if mediated through the guidance service. Other European countries have experimented with various ways in which career counsellors can be used as brokers between supply and demand in adult education (Go-Between II Project, 2002).

# CHAPTER 10. BUILDING POLICY FRAMEWORKS FOR LIFELONG GUIDANCE

This chapter outlines the key challenges that face policy-makers in designing lifelong guidance systems, and sets out the choices that have to be made in translating these challenges into practical programmes.

The chapter's key policy conclusions are that:

♦ There is no one common design for lifelong guidance systems. These will vary according to national traditions and administrative arrangements, and according to the stage of development of career guidance services. However in all countries policy-makers face common choices in designing lifelong guidance systems.

♦ In designing lifelong guidance systems, countries must translate the need for wider access to services, and for a broader focus upon the development of career self-management skills, into practical sets of priorities and specific decisions about how resources are used. In broad terms, the first priority should be for systems and programmes that develop career self-management skills and provide high quality and impartial career information. Policies should not be based upon the assumption that everybody needs intensive personal advice and guidance, but should seek to match levels of personal help, from brief to intensive, to personal needs and circumstances.

♦ A key step is to identify gaps in services. These will differ from country to country. They will depend upon national demographic, economic or economic issues.

♦ Policy-makers need to decide: when the career guidance process should start; how long it should continue throughout life; how responsibility for young people should be shared at key decision points such as the transition from school to work or to tertiary education; whether to deliver services through specialised occupational and organisational structures that provide only career guidance, or to attempt to combine career guidance with other forms of personal services; whether services should be all-age or age-specific; and what mix of present models and more innovative approaches, of the sort outlined in this report, to use to deliver career guidance for adults.

♦ The report concludes with six major issues that need to be considered in designing improved lifelong guidance systems in OECD countries.

*Key challenges in implementing lifelong learning and active labour market policies...*

Chapter 1 set out key challenges for the organisation and delivery of career guidance services that face policy-makers in OECD countries in implementing lifelong learning and active labour market policies. In brief, these are to:

- Move from an approach that emphasises assistance with immediate occupational and educational decision-making to a broader approach that also develops people's ability to manage their own careers: developing career planning and employability skills; and

- Find cost-effective ways to expand access to career guidance throughout the lifespan.

*...need to be translated in practical ways into lifelong guidance systems.*

We have termed the systems that translate these key challenges into practical programmes "lifelong guidance systems". In Chapter 1 a number of features of such systems were described. These are:

- transparency and ease of access over the lifespan, including a capacity to meet the needs of a diverse range of clients;

- particular attention to key transition points over the lifespan;

- flexibility and innovation in service delivery to reflect the differing needs and circumstances of diverse client groups;

- processes to stimulate regular review and planning;

- access to individual guidance by appropriately qualified practitioners for those who need such help, at times when they need it;

- programmes to develop career-management skills;

- opportunities to investigate and experience learning and work options before choosing them;

- assured access to service delivery that is independent of the interests of particular institutions or enterprises;

- access to comprehensive and integrated educational, occupational and labour market information; and

- involvement of relevant stakeholders.

The examples included in this report show that many OECD countries can demonstrate some of these features. However none can claim to have put all of the pieces of the lifelong guidance jigsaw together. Some have more pieces on the table than others. Completing the puzzle will require, in all countries, a significant shift in mindset which policy-makers should not under-estimate.

*Systems will be different in each country. However common choices face all policy-makers.*

In designing lifelong guidance systems there is no single or optimal solution. Policy-makers, in government and elsewhere, must make a number of choices. The types of choices that they make will reflect a number of factors. These include the stage of development of their career guidance systems,[1] their traditions and existing institutional arrangements, and the human and financial resources that are available. And so lifelong guidance systems might take many forms. However there are a number of common choices that must be faced by policy-makers in designing them. It is more helpful to focus upon these choices, and suggest what some of the options associated with them might be, than to try to suggest a single, common model for a lifelong guidance system.

*The broad priorities should be for systems that develop career self-management skills and that provide information.*

## Deciding on broad priorities

This report began by pointing out that traditionally, and still in most cases, career guidance has been a personal service that concentrates upon helping people to make career decisions through personal, face-to-face interviews. A key challenge for policy-makers is to shift their career guidance systems to adopt a broader perspective, emphasising the promotion of people's capacity to manage their own careers. This is consistent with the view that the role of governments in democratic societies is to help citizens to manage their own lives, not to manage their lives for them.

*Policies should not be based upon the assumption that everybody needs intensive personal career guidance.*

This perspective on what career guidance should be trying to do has major implications for the broad priorities that should be adopted in designing lifelong career guidance systems, and in allocating resources within them. Policies should assume that all people need career decision-making skills and career self-management skills, and that everybody needs access to high quality, impartial career information. Accordingly, the first priorities for policy-makers should be systems that develop skills and systems that provide information. Policies should not be based upon the assumption that everybody needs intensive personal advice and guidance, but should seek to match levels of personal help, from brief to intensive, to personal needs and circumstances.[2]

*This has major implications for resource allocation decisions.*

When deciding what to allocate resources to, policy-makers should give the highest priority to activities and resources that develop the capacity to self-manage, and that provide the basis of informed decision making. Examples include: embedding career education in the school and tertiary education curriculum; developing associated resources such as the Real

---

1. Broadly, career guidance systems can be thought of as developing through three stages: an approach that focuses predominantly upon the provision of information; an approach that focuses upon diagnosis and advice giving, so that the person is "matched" to suitable occupations or courses; and an approach that includes an emphasis upon the development of career-management and employability skills. Countries differ widely in the extent to which each of these three stages is evident in their career guidance systems.

2. The existence of a market for career information in many countries reinforces the value that people attach to information as the basis of informed decision making. In Chapter 5 evidence that only a minority of people seem to need extensive personal career guidance was referred to.

Game; introducing programmes that allow people to experience occupations and courses before making decisions; building networks of career mentors; workshops and training courses that teach career self-management skills; producing self-help resources, including those that are ICT-based; introducing open-access resource centres; improving the integration and co-ordination of different types of career information; improving the user-friendliness of career information; and linking career information databases to self-assessment and decision making tools.

*A key step is to identify gaps, and to decide which of these should be priorities. Gaps will vary from country to country.*

### Identifying gaps and priorities

A key step must be to identify gaps in services. Decisions are then needed about priorities in filling these gaps. Gaps in services will vary from country to country. In some cases – for example Ireland – an obvious gap is the relatively weak emphasis that is placed upon a curriculum-based approach within schools. In other countries – for example Austria – the fact that career education is focused upon a limited number of school grades rather than being more widely spread throughout the K-12 curriculum might be seen as a gap. In many countries a gap exists in the lack of effective and well targeted career guidance for young people who have dropped out of school before completing upper secondary education or the equivalent, and who are on the margins of both learning and work. For example in the Czech Republic career education is relatively well embedded in the curriculum, but services for out-of-school youth are weaker. In Ireland these gaps for young people appear to be reversed. Again using the example of Ireland, career guidance within tertiary education might not seem to be a gap, since services are relatively well developed when compared to many other countries. However in a country such as Spain career guidance services in tertiary education might be viewed as a gap, particularly in light of the relatively large size of the tertiary education sector and the relatively high unemployment rates of recent graduates. In virtually all countries services for adults are less well developed than are services for young people. And within the adult population there are particular gaps in services for employed adults wishing to develop their careers, and in services for those on the threshold of retirement. In all countries, the absence of any meaningful data on the size of the private market for career guidance constitutes a gap. An additional gap that is apparent in many countries is the poor co-ordination of career information services: between labour and education portfolios, between different sectors of education, and between different levels of government (see Chapter 6).

*Some gaps will reflect national demographic, educational or economic issues.*

In many countries what are perceived as gaps in services, and the priorities for filling them, will be a function of national demographic, educational and economic issues: for example the existence of refugee and immigrant groups who are not well integrated into the labour market or education has been a factor in the creation of new types of career guidance services in Ireland. In a country such as Spain relatively low rates of female labour force participation and the need for career guidance services to be a tool in helping to raise these might influence decisions on priorities in a way that might not be the case in a country such as Denmark, where female labour force participation rates are higher. The Czech Republic has given a priority to career guidance within schools as part of its national strategies to deal with youth unemployment. The United Kingdom and Ireland have given priority to new services for adults as part of their efforts to improve levels of educational achievement and attainment, particularly among the lowest qualified.

*Resource decisions will flow from the identification of gaps.* Linked to the identification of gaps and decisions about priorities are decisions about methods and resources. As Chapter 5 has indicated, policy-makers have a wide range of delivery methods and tools available to use. Lengthy face-to-face interviews with highly qualified staff are relatively costly, but might be appropriate for those with the greatest needs. Other tools can be included in the repertoire of policy responses, and the mix of these can be tailored to particular types of clients and particular needs: group interviews; ICT or web-based services; self-help tools; open-access resource centres; telephone-based services; services delivered by support staff; organised networks of community members; and curriculum-based services. The choice of the mix of these will influence decisions about the level of resources required. At the same time the resources available will influence decisions on the mix of services to be provided. This reinforces the need for better data on the relative costs of different interventions to better enable such choices to be made.

---

Box 10.1. **A model for comprehensive guidance planning in tertiary education**

Hakulinen and Kasurinen (2002) have proposed a seven-dimensional model to assist the planning of guidance services in the Häme Polytechnic in Finland. The aim of the model is to make the best use of existing resources to meet demands for guidance services and the needs of different client groups during the different phases of an individual learning programme. The seven dimensions are:

**Time:** This refers to the different phases of the individual learning programme: pre-entry, entry, on-programme, exit, and follow-up.

**Content:** This refers to the focus of the service at different points in the student's study programme. For example: enrolment, orientation, selection of a course, or placement.

**Area:** This refers to the groups of staff within the institution (for example qualified staff, trained support staff) who are responsible for different types of services (for example career guidance, personal guidance, educational guidance).

**Location of services:** This describes the division of responsibilities, at different phases of the individual learning programme, between faculty staff members and specialised student services.

**Methodology:** This describes the methods used to meet the needs of different types of clients. For example face-to-face services, group counselling, self-help, ICT, portfolios.

**Systemic:** Where local policies are developed, this describes factors such as the contexts, the development of curricula, the extent to which individual programmes are possible, and how faculties support individuals.

**Context:** This describes the impact upon services of factors such as national policy on guidance, legislation, and national curriculum guidelines.

---

*Lifelong guidance systems require a number of common questions to be addressed by policy-makers.*

A number of other key choices need to be made by policy-makers in building lifelong guidance systems. These include answers to questions such as:

- When should the process start, and how long should it continue?

- How should responsibility for career guidance of young people be shared or divided at the key interface points (compulsory to post-compulsory; secondary to tertiary; education to work)?

- Should career guidance services be structured on an all-age or an age-specific basis?

- Should they be structured on a career-specific or a holistic basis?

- Who should be responsible for services to adults?

Choices such as these can arise at the institutional level as well as nationally. Box 10.1 illustrates how one tertiary education institution in Finland has developed a framework for service planning that attempts to take into account factors such as those discussed above.

*When should the process start...*

### When should the process start?

Traditionally, career guidance services have been concentrated largely around the point at which students leave school. As the age of school-leaving has been postponed, and the educational choices made within the school system have assumed greater importance, the tendency has been for guidance to start just before the age at which students are first required to make educational decisions that have significant vocational implications. Now, however, within the context of lifelong learning, the attention is shifting to helping students to develop the skills and competencies which will enable them to manage their learning and work throughout life. This is a process which can and should start early in primary schools, with, for example, programmes to help pupils to manage their learning and to explore the world of work. Chapter 3 has discussed some of the implications of this for the organisation and management of schools.

*...and how long should it continue?*

Within the context of active employability policies, there are good arguments, outlined in Chapter 4, for career guidance extending to the point at which people are contemplating retirement. A closer integration between financial planning and career guidance would help to ensure more flexible transitions between full-time work and retirement.

*How should responsibility for career guidance for young people be shared: ...*

### Responsibility for young people at key interface points

The issue of who should have responsibility for career guidance of young people has been discussed in Chapter 3. There are three main options that apply to the interface between initial education and work:

- For educational institutions to be responsible.

- For an external agency to be responsible.

- For responsibility to be shared between educational institutions and an external agency.

*…for those in school…*

As discussed in Chapter 3, the first option tends to have weak links with the labour market and can pose problems regarding impartiality. The second tends to have weak links with the curriculum and seems less likely to adopt a skills-development approach, but to focus upon immediate decision-making. There are, then, strong arguments in favour of the major career guidance services for young people who are in initial education being a shared responsibility: between schools and external agencies that have good labour market links and can provide advice which is independent of the needs of the institutions. Such a model requires good co-ordination between education and labour portfolios, and between schools and external agencies, in order to avoid gaps and overlaps.

*…in tertiary education…*

In planning services for young people, another important point of interface is between schools and tertiary education. As indicated in Chapter 3, governments have an important role here in collecting, systematising and distributing impartial information about tertiary study opportunities. They also have an important responsibility to make sure that it reflects consumer needs: for example through providing information on student satisfaction and outcomes, not just on entry requirements and course content. A key issue for tertiary career guidance services is to ensure that they are impartial, not driven by the self-interest of individual institutions, particularly where institutions are competitive and funding is driven by student numbers. Governments should also try to ensure that tertiary career guidance services are comprehensive: encompassing not only advice at the point of enrolment, but also career-management and the development of employability, links between students and future employers, and job placement. A range of levers can be used. Among these are: review, analysis and debate; performance contracts; and the consumer pressures arising from a more diverse and competitive tertiary education environment.

*…and for those not in the labour market?*

Services for young people must also meet the needs of those who have dropped out of education without completing upper secondary school, and who are either unemployed or not in the labour market. All existing examples show that services for this group of young people need to be flexible, part of broader re-insertion programmes that can link them to a range of other services, and managed at the local level. Both government agencies and community organisations have a role to play in the delivery of such services. Careful co-ordination between education and labour authorities is needed to ensure that career guidance for such youth has both a learning and an employment dimension, and can provide personal support and action planning.

*Should services be all-age or age-specific?*

## All-age or age-specific career guidance services?

If services are provided at least in part by external agencies, this opens up the issue of whether such agencies should be structured on an all-age or age-specific basis. The Federal Employment Service in Germany, Luxembourg's ADEM-OP, Careers Scotland and Careers Wales in the United Kingdom are examples of all-age services (although it should be noted that within both the German Federal Employment Service and Careers Wales, services for the two groups are provided by different specialists). On the other hand the Connexions service in England is an external agency providing services to schools and colleges which concentrate upon young people.

Age-specific services enable attention to be focused on the distinctive needs of the age-group in question. On the other hand all-age services can also do this, but at the same time they have a number of organisational and resource-use advantages. In particular they allow a diverse range of services to be provided throughout the lifespan within the one organisational framework. Potentially this allows them to be more cost-effective, avoiding unnecessary duplication of resources. Box 10.2 illustrates many of these advantages.

---

### Box 10.2. **Careers Wales**

In April 2001 the National Assembly for Wales launched Careers Wales, an all-age career guidance service that operates through a confederation of seven regional careers companies with a common brand name. Careers Wales' vision statement sees career guidance as being at the heart of social and economic prosperity, and its mission statement reflects a belief in the development of people through lifelong career planning. Careers Wales is responsible for delivering the statutory careers service for youth, adult guidance, the learndirect call centre network, the Youth Gateway (a short, intensive transition skills course for 16-17 year-olds at risk in the transition from school), and education-business links.

Career education and guidance is seen as a universal entitlement for all young people in Wales. Within the framework of a universal entitlement, some staff specialise in working with those young people who have special needs. Careers Wales supports school and college career education programmes (which are mandatory in Wales for those aged 13-19) through curriculum consultancy, teacher training, and support for careers libraries. Some staff specialise in supporting schools and colleges in this way, and some in providing personal career guidance. An awards process, benchmarked against quality standards, is being used to improve the quality of school and college careers programmes. Through its responsibility for education-business links Careers Wales manages work experience, enterprise education, and mentoring programmes. Each involves both employer support, including quality assurance checks, and teacher development.

All careers companies operate one-stop-shops, and these are accessible on a drop-in basis to all ages. Some adult services are delivered, using an outreach model, in a wide variety of community settings, some through the offices of the individual careers companies, some using a mobile facility, some by telephone, and some online. Careers Wales operates an on-site service within enterprises to assist those facing redundancy. For unemployed 16-17 year-olds Careers Wales provides an employment, education and training referral and placement service.

Staff employed by Careers Wales can work with both youth and adults, but tend to specialise in one or the other. However the fact of a common employing authority for all staff gives service managers flexibility to deploy staff across different areas of specialisation. It is common, for example, for adult guidance staff to spend time in the Welsh learndirect call centres. A single employing authority within an all-age service also gives staff the possibility of a more varied work role.

---

*Should they deal with a range of issues, or provide specialised career guidance?*

*Broad guidance services or specific career guidance services?*

Some age-specific services, particularly those designed for young people, also adopt broad approaches to guidance, helping people with a wide range of personal and social needs, extending beyond career choice and career development. Such "holistic" services can make it easier to take account of the interaction between different parts of an individual's life. Often, for example, it is argued that educational and vocational issues are closely linked to other personal and social issues, and it is difficult to deal adequately with the former without also addressing the latter. (This, of course, is something that is familiar to well-trained career guidance specialists, and can be handled through training in diagnostic skills and through effective referral systems).

On the other hand, as pointed out in Chapter 3, the universal experience is that within a broad or holistic model,[3] career guidance for the wider student body gets squeezed by the more immediate and demanding personal and study problems of those experiencing particular difficulties. There is also a risk within such a model that insufficient attention will be given to the distinctive skills and resources required for career guidance work, including up-to-date knowledge of changes in the education system and the labour market. This report has argued, in Chapter 7, that policy-makers should shift from providing career guidance through occupations composed of shared roles, one of which is career guidance, to providing it through separate, and specialised, occupations with their own appropriate training and qualifications arrangements. These arguments in favour of providing career guidance through separate, specialised occupations and through specialised career guidance services are reinforced by the need, discussed in Chapter 8, for policy-makers to make career guidance services more transparent and visible as part of the process of better specifying supply and demand.

*Some strategies for widening adult career guidance involve policy-makers grappling with quite new approaches.*

*Responsibility for adult career guidance*

A number of broad strategies for extending career guidance to adults have been discussed so far. Each of these could involve policy-makers grappling with quite new approaches to career guidance. In Chapter 4, the possibility of widening access through a restructured role for public employment services was raised, as well as ways of using more extended local partnerships. Chapter 4 also argued for a closer link between financial planning and career guidance in order to encourage more flexible approaches to managing the transition between full-time work and retirement. Chapter 5 outlined how more innovative and cost-effective service delivery methods could be used to increase access to career guidance. It discussed what the implications of these newer delivery

---

3.     Such as found, for example, in schools in Australia (Queensland), in many schools in Canada, in Ireland's upper secondary schools, in Norway's schools, and in the specialised psycho-pedagogical services in the Czech Republic, Luxembourg and Spain

methods might be for how the work of career guidance is organised, including staffing structures, training and qualifications. And Chapter 8 discussed some of the steps that governments might take in to extend market-based models, including making markets more transparent through a better specification of supply and demand, and adopting more innovative approaches to financing career guidance.

*In addition, a number of existing models exist:*

Under current arrangements, policy-makers are faced with four broad models for providing career guidance for adults. Each has advantages and disadvantages.

*Services located within education...*

The first is to locate career guidance services for adults within the education system. This is common in many countries, whether in specialised adult education institutions, as in Austria, Denmark and Spain for example, or in all-age institutions such as Australia's TAFE colleges and Canada's community colleges. Having career guidance services located within educational institutions can help students to see the links between learning and career choices more clearly, and to appreciate that learning is a resource that can be returned to later in life. It also is a more practical solution to the career guidance needs of those having problems mid-course than requiring them to consult an external agency.

On the other hand it can over-identify learning with formal education, emphasise learning at the expense of work, and have weak links with the labour market. Potentially it can also carry the risk, as with career guidance for young people that is located within educational institutions, of advice on enrolment and drop-out decisions being tailored to the interests of the institutions, at the expense of the interests of the individual. There is the additional risk, again as with such career guidance services for young people, that career guidance can take second place to services intended to deal with students' personal, emotional or study problems. And locating career guidance services for adults within educational institutions leaves open the question of where adults who are not in the education system can obtain career guidance.

*...within the labour market...*

A second choice is to adopt a labour-market-based model. This can involve the main services for adults being located within the public employment service. The main current example of such an approach is Germany. However as we have seen in Chapter 4, whilst in nearly all countries the public employment service plays a major role in providing career guidance to some adults, this is generally limited to the unemployed or other selected groups, and the career guidance needs of those who are either employed or not in the labour market are rarely well catered for. Locating career guidance services for adults within employment services can, of course, ensure that career guidance is strongly informed by the needs of the labour market, and also that it is independent of the interests of particular educational institutions and employers. And certainly labour authorities have a strong role in the production and dissemination of occupational and labour market information, for adults as well as young people, in all countries. On the other hand locating the main career guidance services for adults within public employment services, as they are currently organised, may run the risk of career guidance being focused too narrowly upon short-term employment goals, neglecting longer-term career development and planning.[4]

The review has shown that other forms of employment-based career guidance can be influenced by public policy. An example is the use of trade union representatives to provide some initial guidance and access to learning, particularly for low-qualified workers. Other examples include allowing career guidance expenditure to be allowable against training levies, and voluntary quality-mark schemes to encourage enterprises to develop their human resources. Such programmes are described in Chapter 4.[5]

*...within the community...*
A third option, which is illustrated most clearly in Canada, is to rely upon community-based services. This has the potential advantage, as pointed out both in Chapter 4 and in the discussion of funding methods in Chapter 8, of making services more accessible, and in particular of bringing them closer to the needs of target groups that are of particular concern to policy-makers such as the low-qualified, single parents, ex-offenders, and migrants and refugees. However as community-based organisations tend to be quite fragmented, such a strategy runs the risk that many people will fall through the net. It can bring with it a risk of considerable variation in the quality of service provision if it is associated with highly devolved subcontracting as a financing method. As a result the community-based model needs to be linked to quality assurance procedures such as those discussed in Chapter 9, or with performance contracts of the sort used in England's adult information, advice and guidance partnerships which require staff to have specified qualifications and service delivery organisations to meet agreed quality standards.

*...and market-based services.*
The fourth main option for the provision of adult career guidance that can be seen in existing services is a market-based model, in which employers and most adults are expected to pay for career guidance, with government confining its role to the provision of information and to providing guidance for those who cannot be expected to pay for it (notably the unemployed). The Netherlands has perhaps gone furthest in this direction, though a number of other countries have expressed some policy interest in it too. From a public policy stance a market-based model can have the advantage of allowing public expenditure to be targeted upon those most in need, and consequently of allowing career guidance to be provided to a higher number of those in specified target groups. However as was noted in Chapter 8, there seem, in many countries, to be considerable barriers to the

---

4.     However this risk might be less of a concern for the types of broader approaches to career guidance within public employment services that were outlined in Chapter 4.

5.     Development reviews are another form of labour market-based career guidance. They can have the advantage of being systematic and regular, and of focussing upon longer-term planning. However if they are part of employers' appraisal systems they can be seen as an external imposition upon the employee rather than a matter of choice.

introduction of full-cost market-based services without significant changes to the visibility and quality of career guidance, and to how it is financed. And market-based services cannot be a general solution to adults' career guidance needs, as many of those who most need career guidance are least able to afford it.

*A comprehensive approach needs to draw upon all of these…*

The above discussion helps to illustrate the point that none of the major current major models of providing career guidance for adults can meet all needs. One option is to establish new types of services. This can be an attractive option. Normally it requires strong public and political support. And it can be made difficult by resistance from existing interests. In such circumstances policy-makers might prefer to consider how a comprehensive approach can be achieved through a combination of some or all of the existing models discussed above, together with some of the more innovative approaches discussed elsewhere in this report. The need, in the process, to consider questions such as gaps in services, priorities and resources, reinforces the importance of improved national strategic co-ordination of career guidance services that was discussed in Chapter 9, a need which applies to services for both young people and adults.

*…strengthening the case for improved strategic co-ordination.*

---

### To conclude

The creation and management of lifelong guidance systems require policy-makers to address six major issues, whether in considering career guidance services for young people, for adults, or for both. In most OECD countries these issues have, to date, received minimal attention. They are:

- Ensuring that resource allocation decisions give the first priority to systems that develop career self-management skills and career information, and that delivery systems match levels of personal help, from brief to extensive, to personal needs and circumstances, rather than assuming that everybody needs intensive personal career guidance.

- Ensuring greater diversity in the types of services that are available and in the ways that they are delivered, including greater diversity in staffing structures, wider use of self-help techniques, and a more integrated approach to the use of ICT.

- Working more closely with career guidance practitioners to shape the nature of initial and further education and training qualifications in support of the development of career self-management skills, better career information, and more diverse service delivery.

- Improving the information base for public policy-making, including gathering improved data on the financial and human resources devoted to career guidance, on client need and demand, on the characteristics of clients, on client satisfaction, and on the outcomes and cost-effectiveness of career guidance.

- Developing better quality assurance mechanisms and linking these to the funding of services.

- Developing stronger structures for strategic leadership.

# REFERENCES

AUTOR, D.H. (2001), "Wiring the labor market", *Journal of Economic Perspectives*, Vol. 15 (1), pp. 25-40.

AZRIN, N.H., PHILIP, R.A., THIENES-HONTOS, P. and BESALEL, V.A. (1980), "Comparative evaluation of the Job Club programme with welfare recipients", *Journal of Vocational Behavior*, 16, pp. 133-145.

AZRIN, N.H., PHILIP, R.A., THIENES-HONTOS, P. and BESALEL, V.A. (1981), "Follow-up on welfare benefits received by Job Club clients", *Journal of Vocational Behavior*, 18, pp. 253-254.

BEZANSON, L. and KELLETT, R. (2001), "Integrating career information and guidance services at a local level", paper prepared for the OECD Career Guidance Policy Review, *www.oecd.org/edu/careerguidance*.

BOUQUIN, S. (2001), "The point of view of the users of public services: from unemployment emergency to the lifelong learning", paper delivered to a seminar on Innovations in Employment and Vocational Training Services, Charleroi.

BREUNIG, R., COBB-CLARK, D.A., DUNLOP, Y. and TERRILL, M. (2003), "Assisting the long-term unemployed: results from a randomised trial", *The Economic Record*, 79, pp. 84-102.

CABINET OFFICE (2002), *In Demand: Adult Skills in the 21st Century*, London.

CANADIAN CAREER DEVELOPMENT FOUNDATION (2000), *Making Waves: Career Development and Public Policy*, Canadian Career Development Foundation, Ottawa.

CANADIAN CAREER DEVELOPMENT FOUNDATION (2002), *Making Waves: Volume 2. Connecting Career Development with Public Policy*, Canadian Career Development Foundation, Ottawa.

CENTRE DE CO-ORDINATION DES PROJETS D'ÉTABLISSEMENT (2002), *L'Orientation et le tutorat au cycle inférieur dans le cadre des projets d'établissement*, Ministère de l'Éducation nationale, de la Formation professionelle et des Sports, Luxembourg.

COMMISSION OF THE EUROPEAN COMMUNITIES (2001), *Making a European Area of Lifelong Learning a Reality*, Brussels.

DEPARTMENT FOR EDUCATION AND EMPLOYMENT (1998), *The Learning Age*, HMSO, London.

DEPARTMENT FOR EDUCATION AND SKILLS (2003), *Challenging Age: Information, Advice and Guidance for Older Age Groups*, London.

EDWARDS, A., BARNES, A., KILLEEN, J. and WATTS, A.G. (1999), *The Real Game: Evaluation of the UK National Pilot*, National Institute for Careers Education and Counselling, Cambridge.

EUROPEAN COMMISSION (1998), *From Guidelines to Action. The National Action Plans for Employment*, D/98/6, Brussels.

EVANS, J.H. and BURCK, H.D. (1992), "The effects of career education interventions on academic achievement: a meta-analysis", *Journal of Counselling and Development*, 71, pp. 63-68.

FORD, G. (1997), *Career Guidance for the Third Age: a Mapping Exercise,* NICEC Project Report, Careers Research and Advisory Centre, Cambridge.

GAZIER, B. (ed.) (1999), *Employability: Concepts and Policies*, Report 1998, Institute for Applied Socio-Economics, Berlin.

GENERAL ACCOUNTING OFFICE (1999), *Welfare Reform: Assessing the Effectiveness of Various Welfare-to-Work Approaches*, Washington, DC.

GINZBERG, E. (1971), *Career Guidance: Who Needs It, Who Provides It, Who Can Improve It*, McGraw-Hill, New York.

GO-BETWEEN II PROJECT (2002), *The Career Counsellor as a Broker between Demand and Supply in Adult Education*, Careers Europe, Bradford.

GRUBB, W.N. (2002a), "Who am I: the inadequacy of career information in the information age", paper prepared for the OECD Career Guidance Policy Review, *www.oecd.org/edu/careerguidance*.

GRUBB, W.N. (2002b), "An occupation in harmony: the roles of markets and governments in career information and career guidance", paper prepared for the OECD Career Guidance Policy Review, *www.oecd.org/edu/careerguidance*.

GRUBB, W.N. (2003), "The roles of tertiary colleges and institutes: Trade-offs in restructuring postsecondary education", mimeo, OECD, Paris.

GURNEY, R., KINNEAR, P. and CUSACK, M. (2000), *Evaluation of the Career Counselling Programme*, Yarralumla, ACT, Better Enterprises.

HAKULINEN, R. and KASURINEN, H. (2002), "Ohjaus mmattikorkeakouluopiskelijoiden palvelujärjestelmänä – luonnos ohjauksen kehittämiseksi Hämeen ammattikorkeakoulussa" (Guidance as an overall service for students in a polytechnic – a framework for guidance services in Häme polytechnic), mimeo.

HARRIS, M. (2001), *Developing Modern Higher Education Careers Services*, Department for Education and Employment.

HIEBERT, B., McCARTHY, J. and REPETTO, E. (2002), "Professional training, qualifications and skills", in Canadian Career Development Foundation (ed.), *Making Waves: Volume 2. Connecting Career Development with Public Policy*, Canadian Career Development Foundation, Ottawa.

HOLLAND, J. (1997), *Making Vocational Choices: A Theory of Vocational Personalities and Work Environments*, 3rd edition, Psychological Assessment Resources, Inc., Odessa, Fla.

HOUSE OF REPRESENTATIVES STANDING COMMITTEE ON EMPLOYMENT, EDUCATION AND WORKPLACE RELATIONS (2000), *Age Counts: an Inquiry into Issues Specific to Mature-Age Workers,* Parliament of the Commonwealth of Australia, Canberra.

KASURINEN, H. and NUMMINEN, U. (2003), *Evaluation of Educational Guidance and Counselling in Finland*, National Board of Education, Evaluation 5/2003, Helsinki.

KILLEEN, J. (1996a), *Does Guidance Work?: An Evaluation of the Intermediate Outcomes of Gateways to Learning,* Research Studies RS19, HMSO, London.

KILLEEN, J. (1996b), "Career theory", in A.G. Watts, B. Law, J. Killeen, J. Kidd and R. Hawthorn (eds.), *Rethinking Careers Education and Guidance: Theory, Policy and Practice*, Routledge, London, pp. 23-45.

KILLEEN, J. and KIDD, J.M. (1991), *Learning Outcomes of Guidance: A Review of Research,* Research Paper No. 85, Employment Department, Sheffield.

KILLEEN, J. and WHITE, M. (2000) ,*The Impact of Career Guidance on Adult Employed People*. Research Report RR226. Department for Education and Employment, Sheffield.

KILLEEN, J., SAMMONS, P. and WATTS, A.G. (1999), "The effects of careers education and guidance on attainment and associated behaviour", National Institute for Careers Education and Counselling, Cambridge.

KILLEEN, J., WHITE, M. and WATTS, A.G. (1992), *The Economic Value of Careers Guidance*, Policy Studies Institute, London.

KUDER, F. (1977), *Activity Interests and Occupational Choice*, Science Research Associates, Chicago.

LAPAN, R., GYSBERS, N. and SUN, Y. (1997), "The impact of more fully implemented guidance programs on the school experience of high school students: A Statewide evaluation", *Journal of Counselling and Development*, Vol. 75, pp. 292-301.

LAW, B. and WATTS, A.G. (1977), *Schools, Careers and Community,* Church Information Office, London.

LEVIN, H.M. (1983), *Cost-effectiveness: A Primer*, Sage Publications, Beverly Hills, Ca.

McCARTHY, J. (2001), "The skills, training and qualifications of guidance workers", paper prepared for the OECD Career Guidance Policy Review, *www.oecd.org/edu/careerguidance*.

McINTYRE, J.L. and ROBINS, A.F. (1999), *Fixing to Change: A Best Practices Assessment of One-Stop Job Centres Working with Welfare Recipients*, Fiscal Policy Centre, University of Washington.

McMAHON, M. and TATHAM, P. (2002), *Career: More than Just a Job,* Department of Education, Training and Youth Affairs, Canberra.

McMAHON, M., PATTON, W. and TATHAM, P. (2003), *Managing Life, Learning and Work in the 21st Century: Issues Informing the Design of an Australian Blueprint for Career Development*, Miles Morgan, Perth, W.A.

MAGUIRE, M. and KILLEEN, J. (2003), "Outcomes from career information and guidance services", paper prepared for the OECD Career Guidance Policy Review, Paris, *www.oecd.org/edu/careerguidance*.

MARKET AND OPINION RESEARCH INTERNATIONAL (MORI) (2001), *Demand for Information, Advice and Guidance*, The Guidance Council, Winchester.

MARTIN, J. P. (1998), "What works among active labour market policies: Evidence from OECD countries' experiences", *Labour Market and Social Policy Occasional Papers*, No. 35, OECD, Paris.

MEIJERS, F. (2001), "The effects of the marketisation of career guidance services in the Netherlands", *International Journal for the Advancement of Counselling*, Vol. 23, pp. 131-149.

MINISTÈRE DE L'ÉDUCATION QUÉBEC (2001), *Prendre le virage du succès. L'école orientante à l'œuvre : Un premier bilan de l'expérience montréalaise*, Direction de la recherche et de l'évaluation.

MOELLER, G. and LJUNG, V. (1999), "The Korsør production school and the Danish production schools", in OECD, *Preparing Youth for the 21st Century: The Transition from Education to the Labour Market*, Paris.

MORRIS, M., RICKINSON, M. and DAVIES, D. (2001), "The delivery of career guidance in schools", Research Report No. 296, Department for Education and Skills, London.

NATIONAL CENTER FOR EDUCATIONAL STATISTICS (2003), *High School Guidance Counselling*, NCES 2003-15, United States Department of Education, Washington.

NATIONAL CENTRE FOR GUIDANCE IN EDUCATION (2001), Audit of Guidance in Post-primary Schools 1999-2000, National Centre for Guidance in Education, Dublin.

NATIONAL OCCUPATIONAL INFORMATION COORDINATING COMMITTEE (1996), *National Career Development Guidelines K-Adult Handbook*, Washington, D.C.

NATIONAL OCCUPATIONAL INFORMATION COORDINATING COMMITTEE (2000), The NOICC/SOICC Network 1976-2000, Administrative Report No.22, NOICC, Washington, D.C.

OAKES, L. and VON DADELSZEN, J. (2000), "The New Zealand policy framework for career information and guidance", in B. Hiebert and L. Bezanson (eds.), *Making Waves: Career Development and Public Policy*, Canadian Career Development Foundation, Ottawa.

OAKESHOTT, M. (1990), *Educational Guidance and Curriculum Change*, Further Education Unit/Unit for the Development of Adult Continuing Education, London.

OECD (1997), "Responding to new demand in tertiary education", *Education Policy Analysis*, Paris.

OECD (1998a), *Maintaining Prosperity in an Ageing Society*, Paris.

OECD (1998b), *Redefining Tertiary Education*, Paris.

OECD (1999), *The Local Dimension of Welfare-to-Work: An International Survey*, Paris.

OECD (2000a), *From Initial Education to Working Life: Making the Transition Work*, Paris.

OECD (2000b), *Reforms for an Ageing Society*, Paris.

OECD (2000c), *Economic Outlook*, December, Paris.

OECD (2001a), "Lifelong learning for all: Policy challenges", *Education Policy Analysis*, Paris.

OECD (2001b), *The New Economy: Beyond the Hype – The OECD Growth Project*, Paris.

OECD (2001c), *Labour Market Policies and the Public Employment Service*, Paris.

OECD (2001d), *Innovations in Labour Market Policies: The Australian Way*, Paris.

OECD (2001e), *Education at a Glance: OECD Indicators*, Paris.

OECD (2002), "Rethinking human capital", *Education Policy Analysis*, Paris.

OECD (2003a), *Beyond Rhetoric: Adult Learning Policies and Practices*, Paris.

OECD (2003b), "Career guidance: New ways forward", *Education Policy Analysis*, Paris.

OECD (2003c), "Strategies for sustainable investment in adult learning", *Education Policy Analysis*, Paris.

OECD (2003d), "Changing patterns of governance in higher education", *Education Policy Analysis*, Paris.

OFFER, M. (1997), A Review of the use of Computer-Assisted Guidance and the Internet in Europe, National Centre for Guidance in Education, Dublin.

OFFER, M., SAMPSON, J.P. and WATTS, A.G. (2001), *Technology and the Future: Strategic Implications for Higher Education Careers Services of Technically Mediated Service Delivery*, Higher Education Careers Services Unit, Manchester.

OLIVER, L.W. and SPOKANE, A.R. (1988), "Career intervention outcomes: what contributes to client gain?", *Journal of Counselling Psychology*, Vol. 35, pp. 447-462.

PARSONS, F. (1909), *Choosing a Vocation*, Houghton Mifflin, Boston.

PLANT, P. (1998), *New Skills for New Futures: Higher Education Guidance and Counselling Services in Denmark*, FEDORA, Louvain-la-Neuve.

PLANT, P. (2001), "Quality in careers guidance", paper prepared for the OECD Career Guidance Policy Review, *www.oecd.org/edu/careerguidance*.

PRIDEAUX, L., CREED, P., MULLER, J. and PATTON, W. (2000), "A review of career interventions from an educational perspective: Have investigations shed any light?", *Swiss Journal of Psychology*, Vol. 59, pp. 227-239.

ROSEN, S. (1995), "Job information and education", in M. Carnoy (ed.), *International Encyclopedia of Economics of Education*, 2nd edition, Elsevier Science, Oxford.

SAMPSON, J.P., PALMER, M. and WATTS, A.G. (1999), *Who Needs Guidance?*, Centre for Guidance Studies, University of Derby, Derby.

SAMPSON, J.P., PETERSON, G.W., REARDON, R.C. and LENZ, J.G. (1999), "Improving career services through readiness assessment: a cognitive information processing approach", mimeo, Center for the Study of Technology in Counselling and Career Development, Florida State University, Tallahassee, Fla.

SCHILLING, M. and MOIST, A. (1998), *New Skills for New Futures. Higher Education Educational Guidance and Counselling Services in Austria*, report for FEDORA under the Leonardo da Vinci Programme.

SOLESBURY, W. (2001), "Evidence based policy: Whence it came and where it's going", Working Paper No. 1, ESRC Centre for Evidence Based Policy and Practice, *www.evidencenetwork.org/*

SPOKANE, A.R. and OLIVER, L.W. (1983), "The outcomes of vocational intervention", in W.B. Walsh and S.H. Osipow (eds.), *Handbook of Vocational Psychology*, Vol. 2, pp. 99-136, Erlbaum, Hillsdale, N.J.

SUPER, D.E. (1957), *The Psychology of Careers*, Harper and Row, New York.

TEIG, A. (2000), *Skoleradgivning – Status og Utdanningsbehov,* Oslo University College Report 1/2000, Oslo.

THE GUIDANCE COUNCIL (2002), *Creating a Vision for Career Guidance Beyond 2006. Identifying the Research Opportunities,* The Guidance Council, Winchester.

TRICOT, A. (2002), "Amélioration de l'information sur les métiers", paper prepared for the OECD Career Guidance Policy Review, *www.oecd.org/edu/careerguidance*.

VAN WIELE, E. (2003), "'Bijblifrekening', A learning and development account project in Flanders", paper delivered at the ELAP conference, 19-20 May, Berlin.

VUORI, J. and VESALAINEN, J. (1999), "Labour market interventions as predictors of re-employment, job seeking activity and psychological distress among the unemployed", *Journal of Organisational and Occupational Psychology*, Vol. 72, pp. 523-538.

WATT, G. (1996), *The Role of Adult Guidance and Employment Counselling in a Changing Labour Market*, European Foundation for the Improvement of Living and Working Conditions, Dublin.

WATTS, A.G. (2001), "The role of information and communication technologies in an integrated career information and guidance system", paper prepared for the OECD Career Guidance Policy Review, *www.oecd.org/edu/careerguidance*.

WATTS, A.G. and DENT, G. (2002), "Let your fingers do the walking': The use of telephone help lines in career information and guidance", *British Journal of Guidance and Counselling*, Vol. 30, pp. 17-34.

WATTS, A.G. and KIDD, J.M. (1978), "Evaluating the effectiveness of career guidance: A review of the British research", *Journal of Occupational Psychology*, Vol. 51, pp. 235-248.

WATTS, A.G. and VAN ESBROECK, R. (1998), *New Skills for New Futures: Higher Education Guidance and Counselling Services in the European Union*, VUB Press, Brussels.

WATTS, A.G., GUICHARD, J., PLANT, P. and RODRIGUEZ, M.L. (1994), *Educational and Vocational Guidance in the European Community*, Office for Official Publications of the European Communities, Luxembourg.

WHISTON, S.C., SEXTON, T.L. and LASOFF, D.L. (1998), "Career-intervention outcome: A replication and extension of Oliver and Spokane", *Journal of Counselling Psychology*, Vol. 45, pp. 150-165.

WOODS, J. and FRUGOLI, P. (2002), "Information, tools, technology: Informing labour exchange participants", paper prepared for the conference Job Training and Labour Exchange in the U.S., jointly organised by the W.E. Upjohn Institute and the U.S. Department of Labor, Augusta, Michigan, September.

# ANNEX 1. HOW THE REVIEW WAS CONDUCTED

## Participating countries

A proposal to conduct a review of national career guidance policies was approved by the OECD's Education Committee and by its Employment, Labour and Social Affairs Committee in Autumn 2000. Fourteen OECD countries took part in the review: Australia; Austria; Canada; the Czech Republic; Denmark; Finland; Germany; Ireland; Korea; Luxembourg; the Netherlands; Norway; Spain; and the United Kingdom (England, Wales and Northern Ireland).

## National co-ordinators and national questionnaires

Countries taking part in the review appointed a national co-ordinator. Whilst most of these were from key national ministries (education or labour) some were from academic institutions. The national co-ordinators for the review were:

| Country | National Co-ordinator |
|---|---|
| Australia | Ms Robyn Bergin, Department of Education, Science and Training |
| Austria | Dr Gerhard Krötzl, Federal Ministry for Education, Science and Culture |
| Canada | Mr Christian Dea, Human Resources Development Canada |
| Czech Republic | Mr Libor Berny, National Institute of Technical and Vocational Education |
| Denmark | Mr Steffen Svendsen, Danish Institute for Educational Training of Vocational Teachers |
| Finland | Mr Raimo Vuorinen, Institute of Educational Research, University of Jyväskylä |
| Germany | Mr Axel Volhard, Federal Ministry of Education and Research |
| Ireland | Mr Torlach O'Connor, Department of Education and Science |
| Korea | Dr Ji-yeon Lee, Korean Research Institute of Vocational Education and Training |
| Luxembourg | M. Jean Zahlen, Ministère du Travail et de l'Emploi |
| Netherlands | Dr Linda de Ruiter, Ministry of Education, Culture and Science |
| Norway | Ms Annbjørg Rimslåtten, Ministry of Education, Research and Church Affairs |
| Spain | Ilmo. Sr. D. José Luis Mira, Ministry of Education, Culture and Sport |
| United Kingdom | Mr Millar MacDonald, Department for Education and Skills |

In co-operation with national co-ordinators a detailed national questionnaire was developed to obtain details of national career guidance services and policies. The questionnaire included 12 sections:

| | | | |
|---|---|---|---|
| i. | Overview | vii. | Delivery settings |
| ii. | Key goals, influences, issues and initiatives | viii. | Delivery methods |
| iii. | Policy instruments for steering services | ix. | Career information |
| iv. | The roles of the stakeholders | x. | Financing |
| v. | Targeting and access | xi. | Assuring quality |
| vi. | Staffing | xii. | The evidence base |

The national questionnaires sought details of a very wide range of career guidance policies and programmes: in schools; in tertiary education; in the public employment service; in services for adults as well as services for youth; in community-based services; in privately provided services; and in information services as well as services providing advice and guidance. In completing the national questionnaires countries were asked to consult widely with key actors: the major ministries providing or funding career guidance services; state, regional or provincial authorities as well as national authorities; major public and private career guidance service providers; employers and trade unions; organisations representing career guidance practitioners; researchers. In many cases countries formed national steering committees to help them in this task. Generally countries found completion of the questionnaire a relatively lengthy and complex undertaking, with much of the information requested being either difficult or impossible to obtain in many cases. In some countries national co-ordinators assumed the major role in completing the questionnaire. In others it was carried out by the national steering committee working collectively. In further cases the work was contracted out to independent researchers or research organisations.

The completed national questionnaires, together with the other documentation referred to in this annex, can be found on the review's web site: *www.oecd.org/edu/careerguidance*.

**National visits and Country Notes**

Upon the completion of national questionnaires all participating countries received a visit from a review team.[1] During the visit the review team met with national policy-makers, visited career guidance services, met representatives of career guidance practitioners and researchers, and held meetings with key stakeholders such as employers and trade unions. Generally these visits lasted for a week, although in the case of some large countries, and in particular those with federal systems of government, they lasted for a week and a half. In some of the participating countries a national seminar was held as part of the review visit. This enabled key stakeholders to come together with the review team to discuss key policy issues.

Typically the review teams consisted of two people, one from the OECD secretariat and one independent expert. Members of the review teams were:

---

1. With the exception of Finland. Here major reviews of career guidance in the main education sectors and in the public employment service were being conducted at the same time as the OECD review, and it was felt premature to have a national visit before these reviews had been completed.

| Country | OECD secretariat | Independent members |
|---|---|---|
| Australia *(March 2002)* | Mr Tony Watts | Ms Lynne Bezanson, Canadian Career Development Foundation, Canada |
| Austria *(March 2002)* | Mr Richard Sweet | Mr Steffen Svendsen, Danish Institute for Educational Training of Vocational Teachers, Denmark |
| Canada *(July 2002)* | Mr Tony Watts | Ms Annemarie Oomen, National Centre for School Improvement, the Netherlands |
| Czech Republic *(February 2003)* | Mr Richard Sweet | Ms Annemarie Oomen, National Centre for School Improvement, the Netherlands<br><br>Mr Helmut Zelloth, European Training Foundation, Italy |
| Denmark *(January 2002)* | Mr Tony Watts | Mr Raimo Vuorinen, Institute of Educational Research, University of Jyväskylä, Finland |
| Germany *(June 2002)* | Mr Tony Watts | Professor Peter Plant, Danish University of Education, Denmark |
| Ireland *(December 2001)* | Mr Richard Sweet | Mr David Fretwell, The World Bank, United States |
| Korea *(August 2002)* | Mr Tony Watts | Mr John McCarthy, European Commission, Belgium |
| Luxembourg *(June 2002)* | Mr Richard Sweet | Professor Ronald Sultana, University of Malta, Malta |
| Netherlands *(April 2002)* | Mr Tony Watts | Mr Lester Oakes, Careers Service, New Zealand |
| Norway *(February 2002)* | Mr Tony Watts | Ms Lynne Bezanson, Canadian Career Development Foundation, Canada |
| Spain *(September 2002)* | Mr Richard Sweet | Professor Ronald Sultana, University of Malta, Malta |
| United Kingdom *(April 2002)* | Mr Richard Sweet | (Health reasons prevented Professor Peter Plant of the Danish University of Education, Denmark from taking part at the last moment). |

Upon completion of the national visits, brief (25-30 pages) Country Notes were written. These had two aims: to provide a description of national arrangements for career guidance services, largely for the benefit of other countries; and to provide an outline of some of the key policy issues facing the country, as well as some suggestions for how these might be addressed. The latter aim was intended primarily to benefit the country itself.

### Commissioned papers

In association with the European Commission, eight expert papers were commissioned by the review. The papers and their authors were:

| Paper | Author |
|---|---|
| The skills, training and qualifications of guidance workers | John McCarthy, National Centre for Guidance in Education, Ireland |
| An occupation in harmony: The roles of markets and governments in career information and career guidance | Professor W. Norton Grubb, University of California, Berkeley, United States |
| Who Am I? The inadequacy of career information in the information age | Professor W. Norton Grubb, University of California, Berkeley, United States |
| Quality in careers guidance | Professor Peter Plant, Danish University of Education, Denmark |
| Outcomes from career information and guidance services | Malcolm Maguire and John Killeen, National Institute for Careers Education and Counselling, United Kingdom |
| Integrating career information and guidance services at the local level | Lynne Bezanson and Ralph Kellet, Canadian Career Development Foundation, Canada |
| Improving Occupational Information | André Tricot, Institut Universitaire de Formation des Maîtres de Midi-Pyrénées, France |
| The role of information and communication technology in an integrated career information and guidance system | Professor A.G. Watts, National Institute for Careers Education and Counselling, United Kingdom[2] |

### International co-operation

Strong co-operation among international organisations was a notable feature of the review:

- The OECD took an active role in helping to plan the second international symposium on career development and public policy organised by the Canadian Career Development Foundation that was held in Vancouver in March 2001. The inputs to this symposium and its proceedings were an important contribution to the conceptual framework for the review.

- The International Association for Educational and Vocational Guidance (IAEVG) was consulted during the design phase of the review. The IAEVG participated in the initial planning meeting for the activity held in January 2001 in Paris, and as well as in meetings of

---

2.      Professor Watts completed the paper prior to joining the OECD secretariat as a consultant to work on the review.

national co-ordinators held in Paris in January 2002 and in Bonn in September 2002. Progress reports on the activity were given to international conferences of the IAEVG held in Berlin in August 2000, in Warsaw in May 2002, in Wellington in November 2002, and in Berne in September 2003. A progress report on the review was given to the Board of the IAEVG at its meeting in Paris in February 2002. A special issue of the IAEVG's International Journal for Educational and Vocational Guidance in 2004 on comparative studies of career guidance and public policy will include an overview of the review's conclusions and edited versions of some of its commissioned papers.

- As indicated above, the OECD and the European Commission jointly commissioned and funded the eight expert papers commissioned by the review. The European Commission's 2001 Communication on Lifelong Learning (Commission of the European Communities, 2001) identified guidance as a key component of national lifelong learning strategies and as a priority for action. Following its release, the Commission has established a European Expert Group on Lifelong Guidance with a brief to examine issues relating to the provision of lifelong guidance services in the member states and candidate countries in a lifelong learning framework. In preparation for the first meeting of that group, the Commission asked the European Centre for the Development of Vocational Training (CEDEFOP) to gather information on career guidance programmes and policies in those European countries not taking part in the OECD review.[3] The European Training Foundation (ETF) was asked to gather similar data on accession countries.[4] In each case the national questionnaire developed for the OECD review was used to collect data, and the OECD worked closely with CEDEFOP and the ETF to assist in the completion and synthesis of the questionnaires.

- During 2003 the World Bank commenced a review of career guidance policies and programmes in seven Bank client countries.[5] The national questionnaire developed for the OECD review formed the basis of the survey instrument used for the World Bank review, and the OECD participated in the steering group for the Bank review.

- Taken together, the OECD review, the CEDEFOP, ETF and World Bank reviews have resulted in information on national career guidance policies and programmes being gathered against a common framework for 36 countries. This forms a rich set of data for comparative study.

## Dissemination activities

A significant amount of dissemination activity was undertaken in the course of the review to ensure that policy-makers and organisations representing career guidance practitioners were key abreast of the aims of the review and its progress. This took the form of the production of regular newsletters that were electronically distributed to a large international audience, articles in journals and newsletters, and presentations to conferences and seminars. In addition to the presentations to meetings of the IAEVG mentioned above, this activity included presentations to national seminars in Australia, Austria, Denmark, Finland, Greece, Jamaica, and the United Kingdom. A chapter summarising some of the key policy messages from the review was written for the 2003 edition of the OECD's flagship publication Education Policy Analysis (OECD, 2003b).

3.   France, Greece, Iceland, Italy, Portugal and Sweden completed questionnaires.

4.   Questionnaires were completed by Bulgaria, Cyprus, Estonia, Hungary, Latvia, Lithuania, Malta, Poland, Romania, Slovakia and Slovenia.

5.   Chile, the Philippines, Poland, Romania, Russia, South Africa and Turkey.

# ANNEX 2. CAREER EDUCATION IN THE SCHOOL CURRICULUM

| Country | Summary |
|---------|---------|
| Australia | The location of career education in state curriculum frameworks varies. In some cases it is located within personal development, health and physical education syllabuses; in some within social studies; in some it is integrated into a number of subjects across the curriculum. It is also included in courses in work education and the like which are taken by some students but not others. |
| Austria | All grade 7 and 8 students must receive 32 hours of career education each year. In most cases it is integrated into other subjects by normal classroom teachers, many of whom have little training for this. In the *Hauptschule* it is provided as a separate subject in around 45% of cases. |
| Canada | There is very wide variation between and within provinces and territories. For example in British Columbia 60 hours must be devoted to career education and personal planning each year from kindergarten to grade 12 and four credits in this must be obtained for graduation; in Saskatchewan 30 hours of career education are required in grades 6-9; in Ontario a half-credit course in career studies is mandatory in grade 10; in Alberta a grade 11 course in career and life management is compulsory. |
| Czech Republic | Career education is included in the curriculum for all students from grade 7 through to grade 12. Schools may decide whether to teach it as a separate subject or to integrate it into other subjects. In some 25% of compulsory schools it is taught as a separate subject. |
| Denmark | Educational, vocational and labour market orientation is a mandatory topic in grades 1-9. |
| Finland | Career education is compulsory in grades 7-9, and new curriculum guidelines require it to be included in the full basic education. Two hours per week of lessons are provided in grades 7-9, and one hour per week in the optional tenth grade and in upper secondary education. Vocational school students receive 1.5 weeks of career guidance and counselling. The municipalities must provide a comprehensive plan how guidance is delivered as a mainstream service to all and also describe the responsibilities of different actors in a cross-sectoral and multi-professional approach. Additionally the plan must include descriptions of the content and delivery methods of the career education programme which is delivered in separate classes, in individual and group counselling sessions. |
| Germany | Schools incorporate *Arbeitslehre* (learning about the world of work) into the curriculum: either in specific subjects such as technology; or more broadly across the curriculum. It is often in the last two years of compulsory school, but may start much earlier. It is less often taught in the Gymnasium than in other types of schools. Classes are supplemented by work visits, and by work-experience placements. It focuses upon learning about the world of work, rather than upon self-awareness and the development of career planning skills. |

| Ireland | Career education is not mandatory. In upper secondary education two programmes which together account for around 24% of students – the Leaving Certificate (Vocational) and the Leaving Certificate (Applied) – include career education modules. |
| --- | --- |
| Korea | Career education is currently being introduced into the school curriculum. "Employment and career" can be included as an elective "extra-curricular" subject for two hours per week for one semester (*i.e.* a total of 68 hours), both in junior and senior high school. Provinces and schools decide whether it is to be mandatory and how to implement it. |
| Luxembourg | Career education is not mandatory. However some lycées have begun to implement pilot projects, in which career education can be included in grades 7, 8 and 9 for two hours a week. |
| Netherlands | "Orientation towards learning and working" is included in the upper forms of all general subjects, and "orientation towards the sector" in all vocational subjects, within pre-vocational education. Within general education "orientation on continued education" is an optional component within the so-called "free space" periods. |
| Norway | Within the curriculum, the goal is that "educational and vocational guidance shall be interdisciplinary topics regarded as the responsibility of the school as a whole". Teaching about working life is in principle included in the subject syllabuses for each grade within the national curriculum for primary and lower secondary schools, but it tends to be phrased in very general terms. In practice, the main focus is from grade 8 and the extent of such delivery varies considerably: it is estimated that on average it amounts to only perhaps 6 hours in grade 8, 8 in grade 9, and 10 in grade 10, largely concentrated in social studies. |
| Spain | National legislation requires the provision of career guidance throughout the Spanish school and adult education systems. One class hour per week of guidance is included in compulsory primary and secondary education and in the two years of baccalaureate upper secondary education. Both lower and upper secondary vocational education students take a "vocational training and guidance" module for 65 class hours per year, and work experience programmes are a compulsory part of the curriculum in both levels of vocational training. |
| United Kingdom | Since 1997 career education has been a mandatory part of the national curriculum in England for the 14-16 year-old age group, although its extent and content have not been specified and schools have adopted widely differing approaches. Early in 2003 the government announced that career education is to be provided from age 11, and issued guidelines on the learning outcomes to be achieved as part of it. |

# ANNEX 3. THE TRAINING, QUALIFICATIONS AND WORK ROLES OF STAFF PROVIDING PERSONAL CAREER GUIDANCE IN SCHOOLS AND PUBLIC EMPLOYMENT SERVICES

## 1. SCHOOLS

| Country | Training and qualifications |
|---|---|
| Australia | Arrangements differ between the states. For example in New South Wales each secondary school has a full-time careers adviser who must be a qualified teacher and in addition must have either a postgraduate careers qualification or have completed an in-service course. Their work is separate from that of school counsellors, who deal with learning problems and personal difficulties. In Queensland full-time guidance officers combine careers guidance (roughly a third of their time), personal guidance and help with learning problems. They have postgraduate qualifications in educational psychology, which do not necessarily include any specific careers content. In Victoria careers advisers are part-time, combining the role with normal teaching duties. In Western Australia schools make their own decisions on how career guidance is to be provided and on the type of training required and qualifications required of staff |
| Austria | Part-time student advisers are teachers who receive initial training lasting three weeks, followed by six training periods of from one to three weeks each. A standardised initial training course of 208 hours over two and a half years is being piloted in 2003. Student advisers are allocated 1-2 hours per week to provide personal help to students, and this can include career guidance, personal guidance and educational guidance. The work of student advisers can be supplemented by a small School Psychology Service that is staffed by qualified psychologists, and which concentrates upon personal, emotional and study difficulties in addition to career guidance. |
| Canada | Guidance counsellors in most provinces are licensed teachers who usually have a graduate qualification in guidance and counselling at masters level. This may, however, contain little material on career guidance: its main focus is upon personal and social counselling and the remediation of learning difficulties. Generally they are full-time, but the ratio of students to counsellors can be as high as 1:1 200. |
| Czech Republic | Schools employ part-time educational counsellors who are qualified teachers, and whose teaching load is reduced by at most one hour per week in order to perform counselling. They can have a masters degree in psychology or pedagogy, and additional in-service courses are advisable but not compulsory. Approximately 100 schools employ school psychologists, and there is also a network of 94 psychological and pedagogical consulting centres that provide services to schools. Psychologists in both settings mostly provide help with personal and learning difficulties, but may also provide career guidance. They must have a masters level qualification in psychology, but this may not contain any specialised career guidance content. In addition, counsellors of the public employment service provide career guidance to school students. They normally have a qualification in psychology or pedagogy, but this may not contain any specialised career guidance content. |

| | |
|---|---|
| Denmark | One teacher in each *folkeskole* is appointed as a part-time guidance counsellor (for an average of around 20% of their time), and receive a basic training of 240-360 hours. Comparable staff in general upper secondary schools receive 215 hours of training, and those in upper secondary vocational schools 518 hours. Guidance counsellors provide personal and educational guidance in addition to career guidance. |
| Finland | Student counsellors in comprehensive schools and secondary schools are qualified teachers who have also completed a postgraduate qualification at master's level in guidance and counselling. They work as student counsellors on a full-time basis. The qualifications required by student counsellors are specified in national legislation, and may be gained through work-based programmes in addition to formal study. Additional training to doctoral level is available in two Finnish universities. Student counsellors provide personal and educational guidance in addition to career guidance. |
| Germany | The career counsellors of the Federal Employment Service who provide career guidance to school students can undertake a special three-year first-degree course at the service's own *Fachhochschule*, although only around one in five have such a qualification. The rest have normally undertaken a six-month internal course in career guidance. |
| Ireland | Upper secondary schools are allocated one guidance counsellor for every 500 students. They are qualified teachers who have undertaken a one-year postgraduate Diploma in Guidance and Counselling. Their time is divided between classroom teaching of normal school subjects and guidance and counselling, although many are employed full-time on guidance duties. Their work involves personal and educational guidance as well as career guidance. |
| Korea | School counsellors are qualified teachers with (usually) some additional specialist training of 240 hours over one year, leading to a certificate. Some school counsellors have little or no training. Some may have a masters-level qualification. The role includes personal and educational guidance as well as career guidance, and is normally part-time, often for no more than a few hours a week, and rarely for more than two-thirds of their time. |
| Luxembourg | Full-time staff of the Psychology and School Guidance Service (SPOS) work in *lycées* in teams that include a combination of psychologists with (normally) a Bac+4 qualification in psychology, social assistants with a Bac+3 qualification in the health field, and teaching assistants with a Bac+3 qualification in pedagogy. These qualifications need not include material on either guidance and counselling in general or career guidance specifically. SPOS teams provide personal and educational guidance as well as career guidance. In addition to SPOS staff located in the *lycées* there is a specialised support centre, also staffed by qualified psychologists. |
| Netherlands | The Secondary Education Act states that "one or more members of the staff shall be assigned the task of careers teacher/co-ordinator" (section 32). It is however up to the school to decide how this role is defined and how much time and resource are allocated to it. In practice, most if not all schools appoint one or more *schooldekanen*. Some of these have been on a two-year part-time course to train them for their role; some, though, have only been on a course lasting two or three days, or may have had no training at all. |
| Norway | The Education Act states that: "The pupils have the right to necessary guidance on education, careers and social matters". What is "necessary" is, however, largely left to schools to define. In most cases, the service is provided mainly by teachers who function as guidance counsellors and provide both educational/vocational guidance and educational welfare counselling. About half have had "relevant" training (defined very broadly to include, for example, general psychology and sociology) equivalent to half a |

year's study, around a quarter have had less than this, and the remaining quarter had had no relevant training at all. They have a reduced teaching load according to a formula under a collective agreement which provides for a minimum of one hour per 25 pupils.

Spain

Both guidance and counselling departments within schools, and counselling support centres that are located outside schools, are staffed by teams that normally consist of counsellors, teachers and social workers. These teams provide personal and educational guidance in addition to career guidance. Counsellors are required to have a university degree in psychology, pedagogy or educational psychology. These degrees need not contain any content specific to career guidance.

United Kingdom

In England Connexions (previously known as the Careers Service) employs full-time Personal Advisers (some of whom were previously known as Careers Advisers) who work with a range of young people's problems, not only career guidance. However in most Connexions companies career guidance appears to be a full-time and specialised role, and Personal Advisers who concentrate upon career guidance must have a postgraduate qualification in career guidance or its equivalent. In Wales seven specialised Careers Wales companies provide a similar service to schools, and have similar training and qualifications requirements of their staff. In Northern Ireland the Careers Service employs full-time specialised career guidance staff with specialised career guidance qualifications that are essentially the same as those of the staff of Connexions in England and Careers Wales in Wales.

## 2. THE PUBLIC EMPLOYMENT SERVICE

**Country**  **Training and qualifications**

Australia

Employment services are contracted out to a range of non-government organisations, only some of which provide career guidance as part of their range of employment services, and then under no standard conditions. However specialised career guidance is available to clients meeting specified criteria through the Career Counselling Programme, and those who staff this programme are required to have specialised career guidance qualifications, preferably at postgraduate level.

Austria

Career guidance is provided within the offices of the Federal Employment Service (AMS) and through a network of 52 specialised career information centres (BIZ) that are administered by the AMS. AMS staff combine career guidance with other forms of employment assistance such as job placement. All AMS staff undertake an initial six-month full-time internal training course, of which career guidance is one component, and receive an additional one-and-a-half week internal training each year, though this need not be in career guidance.

Canada

As public employment services in Canada are largely devolved to the provinces, and in many provinces career guidance is contracted out to the community sector, there is wide variation in how career guidance is provided within employment services, and in the training and qualifications of those who provide it.

Czech Republic

Specialised information and counselling centres are located within each employment office. They are staffed by counsellors who would normally have a tertiary qualification in psychology or pedagogy, although these need not necessarily include specific career guidance content.

| Denmark | There are separate guidance counsellors and placement officers in the public employment service, although the roles have recently become more blurred: it is accepted that placement officers may offer some basic guidance, and that guidance counsellors may be involved in developing individual action plans. Training for guidance counsellors is in-house, as part of the general training programme for public employment service staff: it comprises a two-week course on top of the basic three-month initial training provided for all staff. This represents a reduction from the former training pattern. |
|---|---|
| Finland | The Finnish Employment Office employs some 280 specialised vocational guidance psychologists. Each has a Masters degree in psychology, and also completes short in-service training. Many obtain further postgraduate qualifications. Their work is separate from job placement. In addition the Employment Office employs educational advisers and employment consultants who specialise in dealing with special needs clients and who run job clubs. |
| Germany | Within the Federal Employment Service career guidance and job placement are combined within the one role in the case of young people, but for adults career guidance constitutes a separate specialisation in its own right. Vocational counsellors can undertake a special three-year first-degree course at the service's own *Fachhochschule*, although only around one in five have such a qualification. The rest have normally undertaken a six-month internal course in career guidance. |
| Ireland | Most Irish Training and Employment Agency (FÁS) Employment Service Officers provide both employment services and career guidance. Close to eight in ten have at least some form of guidance training. Staff are able to undertake the University of Ireland, Maynooth, Certificate in Adult Guidance and Counselling on a part-time basis over a twelve month period. FÁS has set itself the goal of increasing the number of its staff who are qualified at Diploma/Higher Diploma level in guidance and counselling. |
| Korea | The staff of the public employment service include nearly 2 000 vocational counsellors. Many were recruited on the basis of a knowledge-based qualification test set up as part of the National Technical Qualification Test System: passes could be achieved after a course of 1-3 months run by private training institutions. Nearly 27% of vocational counsellors in the public employment security centres currently have this qualification, but around 20 000 people have now passed the test, so it no longer has much market value, particularly as in some of the employment services it is preferred but not mandatory. Currently a "grade 2" test is being introduced for those who have passed the basic test and have acquired five years' experience. Short one-week courses are also run by the Ministry of Labour for recruits on entry and after one year: these are concerned mainly with administrative matters, though the second one includes some career guidance theory. There are plans afoot to move towards a more professional structure of bachelor and masters degrees. |
| Luxembourg | The Employment Administration contains a small, specialised career guidance service. Its staff are generally recruited under normal public service conditions, and are not required to have specific career guidance qualifications. Some, however, have tertiary qualifications in pedagogy or the social sciences. |
| Netherlands | Career guidance is not normally provided directly by the Dutch Centres for Work and Income (CWI), but purchased from a range of private reintegration agencies, although client needs for such services are diagnosed by the CWI. Reintegration companies employ a wide range of specialised staff, including psychologists, careers advisers, work advisers, and reintegration consultants. These staff possess a wide range of qualifications, which would normally be at tertiary level and in a field related to career-management. |

Norway | There are no formal requirements for the counselling staff of the public employment service to have specialised career guidance or counselling qualifications, although this is regarded as desirable. Extensive in-service training is available at four levels.

Spain | Public employment services have, in most instances, been decentralised to the control of the Autonomous Communities. Staff providing career guidance are normally required to have a degree or associate diploma level qualification. This can be in a field such as psychology, but can also be in fields such as law or sociology. Specialised career guidance content need not be included within these qualifications. In-service courses are normally available for public employment service staff, and these can be in career guidance.

United Kingdom | Employment Service/Jobcentre Plus staff attend internal training courses to prepare them for their role, and these courses can include elements of career guidance. Frontline staff are encouraged to undertake qualifications in customer service. Many specialist advisers within Jobcentre Plus have specialised guidance qualifications in addition to internal training. Clients requiring specialised career guidance will normally be referred to a specialised external career guidance agency such as Connexions or an Information, Advice and Guidance for Adults partnership.

# ANNEX 4. ESTIMATES OF TOTAL GOVERNMENT EXPENDITURE ON CAREER GUIDANCE IN THREE COUNTRIES

This annex briefly describes the types of data available in the three countries for whom at least an approximate estimate can be made of the total cost to government of providing career guidance.

### Australia

Responsibility for government funding of career guidance services in Australia is divided between the federal government and the states and territories. The states and territories have constitutional responsibility for education and the federal government is responsible for employment services. While in schools the states have major funding responsibility, in tertiary education the federal government provides the bulk of the funds, through the states. The federal government uses contracting out extensively when funding career guidance services.

For the federal government, estimates are available of the costs within the education portfolio of funding special career guidance programmes and of national career guidance initiatives such as the introduction of the Real Game. In the federal employment portfolio, an estimate can be provided of the costs of providing career information and of relevant labour market analysis. However it is not possible to estimate the costs of providing career guidance through the employment service network, which is contracted out. In addition, an estimate is available of the costs to the federal government of career guidance provided through the defence forces recruiting organisation.

In the case of schools the quality of the data that is available varies between the states. In New South Wales schools have full-time careers advisers, and the cost of their salaries is available, in addition to other costs for special career guidance programmes. In Victoria school funding is highly decentralised, and a consolidated estimate of career guidance staff costs is not possible. However the cost of central funds provided for a tagged career guidance component of a managed individual pathways programme is known. No data is available for the state of Queensland. In South Australia no data is available on direct staff costs in schools. However the (quite small) costs of regional networks developed to support local careers initiatives are known. For Western Australia, only the costs of career information services are available. However whilst direct salary costs for school career guidance staff are poor in all states except New South Wales, an estimate is available of the number of full-time-equivalent career guidance staff in schools across all states and territories and both public and private school systems. Using average teaching salary costs, this can be translated into an estimate of the costs of career guidance services in schools. (Note however that in the non-government school sector student fees rather than government grants account for a proportion of total expenditure, and thus the estimate provided of total school sector salary costs is likely to slightly over-estimate government costs.)

In tertiary education the number of full-time-equivalent career guidance staff in universities is known, and this can be used, together with average salary costs, to estimate the costs of career guidance services in universities. However it is thought that this might be an under-estimate given the costs of providing career guidance services that were able to be provided directly by selected universities. In the Technical and Further Education sector the number of career guidance staff is known for some states but can at best be estimated in others. Average salary costs in association with staffing estimates have been used to obtain cost estimates.

In summary, much of the Australian data is based upon estimated staff numbers in association with average salary costs, rather than upon direct expenditure data. The major gap is the lack of data on career guidance provided through the contracted-out public employment service.

### Austria

In Austria most government funds for career guidance services are provided directly rather than through contracting out. Relatively complete data is available in Austria for estimating the costs of career guidance provided within schools. Career education lessons are provided for all students in grades 7-8 for 32 lesson periods in each year. Average teaching salaries for these lessons are able to be estimated, as can the additional administrative costs associated with the lessons.

In addition to career education lessons, Austrian schools employ student advisers. These are normal teachers who have had special training for the role, and who are given 1-2 hours per week release from teaching to perform it. They receive an allowance for their work, and the cost of these allowances is available. The administrative costs of their training and the costs of producing special materials for them are also available. However the costs of their release time in order to provide advice to students are not available.

Career education lessons and student advisers are complemented by a small school psychology service which provides career guidance for only some of its time. In addition the service provides training and resource development support to the other two career guidance services within schools. An estimate is available of cost of the proportion of the time that the school psychology service devotes to career guidance, as well as of the cost of the administrative support that it provides.

Tertiary education in Austria is funded directly by central government, and an estimate is available of the personnel and administrative costs of both direct and indirect career guidance services in tertiary education.

Some estimates are available of the costs of providing administrative support to career guidance services in adult education in Austria, but not of the direct costs of these services in adult education institutions.

No estimate is available of the costs of providing direct career guidance services in the labour portfolio, as these costs are included within the costs of providing other employment services such as job placement. However data is available on the cost of some career guidance services that are contracted out to external organisations.

An additional type of career guidance service that is quite important in Austria is the regular careers fairs held in major cities. These are funded by government and by other stakeholders. However no estimate of the costs to government of funding these fairs is available.

In summary the main gaps in the Austrian data which lead to an under-estimate are the lack of data on the costs of the release time of student advisers, exclusion of many costs in the public employment service and the existence of only limited data on costs in adult education institutions.

### England

In England the costs of the Connexions Service, which provides a direct, external career guidance support service to schools are known. However whilst the Connexions Service is a very large provider of career guidance to young people, it also provides other forms of support and advice to youth (for example assistance with housing or drugs issues). Thus government expenditure on the Connexions Service will over-estimate career guidance expenditure in the absence of an estimate of the proportion of resources within Connexions devoted to career guidance compared to other forms of activities. In addition to the Connexions Service, career guidance for young people is provided by schools and Further Education colleges themselves including the career education programmes and the careers libraries that schools and colleges are required by legislation to provide. The costs of both of these are not known.

Government funds for adult career guidance are provided through a set of local adult information, advice and guidance partnerships. The costs of direct government support for these are known. In addition, the government funds career guidance for adults through the learndirect service, and the direct costs of this are known. Some government funds to support career guidance for adults are provided through the Union Learning Fund, but the extent of these funds is not known. Government expenditure, through the labour portfolio, on Worktrain, a major on line career information service, is available. The cost of career guidance provided in the public employment service through the Jobcentre Plus centres is unknown.

The costs of career guidance services in higher education are also unknown.

In summary, the estimate of total costs provided for England is an over-estimate to the extent that Connexions provides services other than career guidance, and an under-estimate through the omission, in particular, of estimates of the costs of career guidance provided directly by schools and the costs of career guidance provided through the local offices of the public employment service.

OECD PUBLICATIONS, 2, rue André-Pascal, 75775 PARIS CEDEX 16
PRINTED IN FRANCE
(91 2004 01 1 P) ISBN 92-64-10564-6 – No. 53367 2004